Prayers From the Altar

From the Heart of A Shepherd

Chief Apostle Dr. J. G. Rice

Chief Apostle Dr. J. G. Rice

Copyright © December 2014 by Chief Apostle Dr. J. G. Rice

All rights reserved.
No part of this book may be reproduced or printed transmitted in any form, or by any means. Electronically, or mechanically, including photocopying, recording, or storage on informational devices, without he expressed or written permission of the copyrighted owner.

ISBN-13: 978-0692349748
ISBN-10: 069234974X

Publishers
Rice Ministries InterGlobal Publishing Company
5570 NW 10th Terrace
Fort Lauderdale, Florida 33473

Mailing Address
P.O. Box 121436
Fort Lauderdale, Florida 33309

Publishers Contact Information
855-200-7729
www.kawebtv.com
www.chiefapostlerice.com

Publishing Company
Mygazine Publications
A division of Hills Management Group LLC
2901 Two Notch Road
Columbia, South Carolina 29204

803-200-1707
www.mygazinepubications.com

To Order Additional Copies of this book, contact
www.greaterharvestchristiancenter.com
www.chiefapostlerice.com

Rice Ministries InterGlobal 1-855-200-7729
ghccstaff.mm@gmail.com

This book was printed in the United States of America

FOREWORD

By Dr. J. G. Rice- Chief Apostle

These prayers were "actually prayed" by Chief Apostle Dr. J. G. Rice a Shepherd that cares, during various service times in the temple of Greater Harvest Christian Center Churches Worldwide, (an IGACCW affiliate). Prayers from the altar, is where a shepherds heart bleeds for the people of God.

They are Prayers of fire, power, deliverance, health, wealth, wisdom, family victory ,worship, praise, celebration, declarations, and much more.

These prayers hold the light of God's word to our lives and allow us to put the armor of God on and equip ourselves for the joyous life of God. Dr. J G Rice (I) am an anointed prayer warrior, believer of decreeing and a communicator with God in prayer. We have prayed all over the country, as well as in Revivals and Conferences led by myself, Chief Apostle Rice, and Arch Bishop James Rice, Gods prophetic Ambassadors. Our heart is open through tears, laying before the Lord, hours in the temple of God and abroad by ourselves, our church leaders and family, and with the 120 prayer warriors interglobally.

It is the desire of my heart that others would be drawn to "Prayer" at all cost. Be it 12 Midnight, 3 am, 6 am, 12 noon, or whenever the Father "bids you to come" and for as often as he bids you to stay and abide in his presence.

We must realize that Prayer is communication with God; we must enjoy waiting on Him. We must desire the Father to take us in like small children and to communicate with Him. I assure you that if you love to pray and communicate with God, the Spirit of the Most High God, will visit you, communing with you in the same greatness of joy, and you will get the answers of the "Learned" and the peace that passes all understanding.

The first 4 chapters are teaching and Impartation. The next 5 sections contains 63 prayers that will bless your life and cause you to become "Gods Ambassador of Prayer." Take a 90 day (3 month) journey with us in Prayer, and see the victory return to your life and your entire being be made strong in the Lord, and the Power of his Might.

Best Effective Way to Use This Prayer Sword

Here's the plan…

Start with the 1st Prayer on your Day One.

Pray it for 3 days and continue on the journey.

Prayer in sequence, one after the other

At the end of the 90 day journey, start over!

Pray and Decree each prayer over your life at least 4 times a year.

This systematic type of prayer covering will put a blood seal over you, your family, and your loved ones.

This puts the power of agreement in action.

REMEMBER you don't have to see me to pray for me!

And most of all, know that you don't have to see us to know that I am, we are, praying for you.

I remain humbled to do so and show you the heart of a Shepherd.

So let's take it to the Lord in prayer, yes let's take it to the Altar, and know I will be at the Altar with you.

Chief Apostle Dr. J. G. Rice
Kingdom Ambassador, Master Prophet, Life Coach, Mentor, University Chancellor, Revivalist, Conference Leader, Author, Psalmist, and Wife, Mother and Friend.

CONTENTS

Introduction	9
Chapter 1	13
Chapter 2	21
Chapter 3	31
Chapter 4	45
Chapter 5	59
Section One Prayers of Affirmation and Declarations	65
A Christians Belief	69
My Morning Declarations	70
Who I Am In Christ	72
I Am A Child of God	73
Affirming the Grace of God to Me	75
Affirming the Promises of God	76
Prayer for the Church and its Vision	78
My Declaration of Victory and Faith for Daily Living	82
Affirmations for My Spiritual Leaders	84
Decree for Growth in Christian Vision	87
Decree of Establishment	91

Affirmations of Great Success	93
Section 2: Prayers of Breakthrough and Warfare	95
Breaking the Spirit of Deceptions	99
Breakthrough Prayer: To Cast Out the Spirit of Deception	101
Daily Prayer to Open the Gateways of Receiving Blessings	103
Breakthrough Prayer for Power of Promotion and Expectation	104
Breakthrough Prayer: The Heavens Will Arise in My Favor	107
Breakthrough Prayer over Difficult Things	109
I Am a Mountain Of Praise: I Confess and Decree These Scriptures	111
Breakthrough Prayer for Promotion	113
Breakthrough Prayer of Greatness for My Year	114
Breakthrough Prayer to Attract Wealth	115
Breakthrough Prayer to Destroy City/Area Blockades	117
Breakthrough Prayer for My Entire Family	118
Breakthrough Prayer for Great Health	121
Breakthrough Prayer to Release and Invoke My Heavenly Impact Team	123
Breakthrough Prayer to Unleash Gods Power for Me	125

Breakthrough Prayer to Overcome All Obstacles	127
Breakthrough Prayer from Stubborn Pursuers	129
Section 3: Prayers of Intercession	131
Prayer to Business, Great Personal Motivational Success and Family Greatness	135
The Prayer of Psalm 91	137
The Healing Decree	140
Prayer to Invoke My Angelic Benefits: Blessings	142
Prayer to Invoke My Angelic Benefits: Deliverance	144
Prayer to Invoke My Angelic Benefits: Promotion	146
Prayer to Invoke My Angelic Benefits: Protection	148
Prayers to Invoke My Angelic Benefits: Waging War against the Enemy	150
Prayers to Invoke My Angelic Benefits: Dislodge Evil	152
Prayers to Invoke My Angelic Benefits: Dismantle Evil Agendas	153
Prayers to Invoke My Angelic Benefits: Dismantling by Fire	155
I Release the Spirit of Rest and Peace on My Journey	157
The Resurrection Power Prayer	161
The Prayer of Public Success	164
Confessions for My Bloodline as an Intercessor	166

Prayer of Spiritual Renewal and Restoration	169
Section 4: Special Forces Prayers of Deliverance, Power and Victory	173
Alerting My Morning and Taking Captive My Day	177
Back To God Prayer	185
Spiritual Warfare Prayer	191
Prayer for My Leaders and the World	193
I Am Chief Apostle, and This is a Time of Prayer	195
I Decree I Have Favor	201
We Decree We Will Come Back To God Prayer	203
Prayer of Thanksgiving	209
Set Us Free and Give Us the Bondage Releasing Anointing	210
Prayer of Evangelism	212
Oh God, Save Them Prayer	214
Prayer for Those In Need of Salvation	217
Rebuking the Curse off Our Families Finances	222
Prayer of Repentance	225
Breaking the Back of the Enemy	230
Prayer for the Author	233
I Seal Every Prayer in the Mighty Name of Jesus	235

NOTES

Chief Apostle Dr. J. G. Rice

INTRODUCTION

There is a time in our life, when we must become spiritually mature; and there are times when we are still unaware of Satan's devices, (please know that this small "s" is by choice) where we should be ahead of his terrible plans of destruction and not believe his folly. This will only happen by our maturity in our prayer life, and constant prayer reinforcement of positive strategic prayers of all types and degrees for all seasons in our lives.

We need help in the realms of Prayer that will take us past the surface and into the Heavens of God. We can no longer be reactive, we must become proactive in prayer! Prayer must become a daily benefit to defeat the enemy afar. Before his attacks, not after as a victim! Be prepared to defeat him in Jesus name.

We are in a time when we have to deal with spiritual warfare in a strategic manner because the enemy, the devil, is a *"creeper."* He will creep in, and if you're not careful, you will find yourself being like Apostle Paul in the scriptures of the Holy Bible saying, "Things I said I wouldn't do, I find myself doing," because you've missed the opportunity to be prayed up in that area. And while you were asleep, with your eyes wide open, the enemy came and stole from you. He sowed tares in your field and he bound up your house, both physically and naturally.

Can I say to you with expressed permission from the Holy Ghost that "Jesus has done all He's going to do." They sang a song when I was in the Apostolic, Pentecostal, Charismatic, Church of God In Christ, (laugh if you can) ... it says, "What More Can He Do? He has laid the foundation and open the way, what more can He do?" Jesus is not going to do anything else until He cracks the sky again! Everything pertaining to Holiness and Godliness, and all that we need to know, is in the Word and will be found in our relationship with him **THROUGH PRAYER!**

Through our verbal, mental, emotional and financial communication with "El The First and The Last" and The Great I Am! We will find EVERYTHING we need! So if we know someone who has all the answers, why do we slight speaking to him and gaining life instructions? This can only be done in PRAYER. Time on the "Altar of God. "Time still speaking with the Father and worshipping will still produce an abundance of His Glory in your life.

Sometimes I personally get into the presence of God and all I can do is moan, cry, rejoice, sing, pray and listen to GOD for hours. I will pray, cry, read His word and rejoice. I can do this over and over! Sometimes I get in His presence and all I can do is laugh. (I know you may not be able to relate to this because you're still stuck on yesterday's prayers and religious actions.) But God is so multifaceted and full of...everything. He wants us to fill His glory and go from Glory to Glory, moving up in Him. We can never think we've reached the "All in God!" No way! Stretch more and get more!

We Must Be Guided to "See Gods Hand Move"

We cannot stay stuck on that old dead non- communicating prayer life. I do apologize that some of my co-labors in the Gospel have NOT shown you, by example, that prayer is needed. When is the last time you heard your leader REALLY pray until Gods hand moved? Sometimes we are so busy for God, that we don't have time to spend with God.

Yes Pastors, we can't just call PRAYER MEETINGS, we must attend them and lead them as well. We cannot stay in the office for Praise and Worship, Devotional time, or Sunday School. A leader must be out front. So examine yourself. Where is your prayer life with GOD? Are you consumed with the Work of God, and have left the Altar of Worship and Prayer? If so, He still loves you too; come back to the ALTAR, yes even the most highly called and anointed need to PRAY!

We Must Push Our Hearts in PRAYER and Get Our Prayer Life On!

Let's be honest, some of the stuff you say is out of tradition. Out of you formulating that old mind set and that's where you're stuck. That's why we need a prayer manual to help get "unstuck" and to be pushed to our Creator and Heavenly Father, and Jesus Christ out Savior in God! Bishop TD Jakes said something very important. He says, **"A stuck person is a betrayer."** Why? Because God is about movement. When a person gets stuck and they realize their stuck, they get angry, mad, upset, and feel defeated. When these feeling start and they can't get free, they are a target for the enemies use.

We Must Be Guided Out of Our Rut Before We Got Stuck!

How do I know when the devils using someone, anyone? Here's the clue… they were once happy and now they begin to complain about everything. They start participating in other ungodly conversations. They start having their mindset shifted from the things and the movement of God. Shifted to unhappy thoughts and pattern of defeat, because they are just stuck. Show me a complaining person, and I will show you a Non-Praying and Non-Atmosphere changing person. Yep! That's what you should look for, the person who is not changing and growing up in CHRIST. Flee from them and run to prayer, for they will soon melt like wax! It's a fact that even your car changes gears when it's driving. We must do the same in the Christian Faith. We must learn how to **GROW UP** and accept Godly and Spiritual changes which will lead to **POWER**.

Others Will Pass By A Car That is Stuck On The Highway of Life

Have others passed by you while you have been stuck in the time of non-movement and unpreparedness? Yes, they have! Why? It's because you refuse to be honest with yourself. Recognize that you are not growing in the grace of God in prayer and in relationship. Until now you may never have even invested in a prayer training book like this one, because you thought, "I know HOW to pray."

We Must Guide You To "Increase Your Rate of Answered Prayers"

Let me ask you something, what is the rate your prayers really get answered? Is that working for you? Well it's time to learn how to pray in FAITH, PUT GODS WORD to WORK FOR US, and We must "Lift up the Prayers" and take it to another level, go higher in God. In other words, **COME ALIVE!** Be excited to talk to God. Be excited to learn new prayer levels and decree them with POWER! Yes, Feel His power and embrace His Love.

You should do this every time you get on your knees. We need to enter in with the fervent of passion before God, a love before God that changes the atmosphere. If we are really honest with ourselves and our prayers, we would admit that very rarely are our prayers changing the atmosphere. But we can change this today with Prayers from the ALTAR, a Shepherds cry. Let this next 90 days put you on an awesome path of Prayer.

By the time you end the Year, you will be so much closer to God. Now you can really start a "Prayer circle" (5 people) dedicated like you to pray every day for 90 days and do these prayers 4 times a Year. Praying effective prayers to keep your family, yourself, Ministry, and lives covered under the Blood of Jesus! Get exciting people, or just do it by yourself knowing corporately others are praying with you as well, all over the Kingdom of God! So it is time to make your move, God is there to meet you with the Fire so let's get on FIRE!

Chapter 1
Why We Need A Prayer Guide Book ?

NOTES

Chapter 1

It's grieving God to know that you are not pressing in, thrusting in, and getting to the next level in Him. You should be improving in prayer, yet the church is failing in prayer. If you are still saying the same thing that you said last year, at the same rate and pace, and in the same time span, then something's wrong. And it's **called "Spiritual Retardation."** I define this as: **The Inability to Grow or Press Pass a Point of Learning.**

We Must Be Guided to "Press In"

You have retarded yourself! If you don't grow in PRAYER, and become graced to know how hoe to pray! A little DAB will NOT do it! It will take relationship time with God in Prayer. Most impaired believers think that they are fine with 3 minutes of prayer. It is common that they think that they/you have finally arrived, yet it is bad to know that your level of growth has not changed in many years. I encourage new believers not to get stuck in the rut of "No Communication with your Heavenly Father." Do not ever train your will, emotions, body, spirit or mind to think that you are so **"Mature in God"** and that you know Him so well that you don't have to seek God for more of Him. Let's go back to the ALTAR in Prayer!

We sang a song just the other night, "I Want More of You God." More means "to increase." I don't want to keep saying the same things over and over again to God. If I had a conversation with you and all I had to say was the same thing over and over you would find me "boring." God is a good Father and of many words. Just look at the Bible. God really can talk… a lot. Look at how He speaks. He is not repetitious. **HE** is so **BIG**! He has 1500 names or more! So we don't even have to call Him the same name over and over again.

We Must Be Guided to "Grow"

God finds your repetitious prayers really vain and religious because you have practiced it. It doesn't even draw a tear to your eyes. It doesn't open you up to where you need to be. It has no power! God wants to be the person in your life that truly touches the Sprit in your body. That touches the Soul in your body. That creates POWER for you, and in you!

Some of us can't even relate to each other in the Spirit of God, or in the Spirit of Truth. We can really learn to stretch out to God, and know that opening up to God will allow us to open up to each other.

Sometimes I personally get into the presence of God and all I can do is moan, cry, rejoice, sing, pray and listen to GOD for hours. I will pray, cry, read His word and rejoice. I can do this over and over! Sometimes I get in His presence and all I can do is laugh. (I know you may not be able to relate to this because you're still stuck on yesterday's prayers and religious actions.) But God is so multifaceted and full of...everything. He wants us to fill His glory and go from Glory to Glory, moving up in Him. We can never think we've reached the "All in God!" No way! Stretch more and get more!

We Must Be Guided to "See Gods Hand Move"

We cannot stay stuck on that old dead non- communicating prayer life. I do apologize that some of my co-labors in the Gospel have NOT shown you, by example, that prayer is needed. When is the last time you heard your leader REALLY pray until Gods hand moved? Sometimes we are so busy for God, that we don't have time to spend with God.

Yes Pastors, we can't just call PRAYER MEETINGS, we must attend them and lead them as well. We cannot stay in the office for Praise and Worship, Devotional time, or Sunday School. A leader must be out front. So examine yourself. Where is your prayer life with GOD? Are you consumed with the Work of God, and have left the Altar of Worship and Prayer? If so, He still loves you too; come back to the ALTAR, yes even the most highly called and anointed need to PRAY!

We Must Push Our Hearts in PRAYER and Get Our Prayer Life On!

Let's be honest, some of the stuff you say is out of tradition. Out of you formulating that old mind set and that's where you're stuck. That's why we need a prayer manual to help get "unstuck" and to be pushed to our Creator and Heavenly Father, and Jesus Christ out Savior in God! Bishop TD Jakes said something very important. He says, **"A stuck person is a betrayer."** Why? Because God is about movement. When a person gets stuck and they realize their stuck, they get angry, mad, upset, and feel defeated. When these feeling start and they can't get free, they are a target for the enemies use.

We Must Be Guided Out of Our Rut Before We Got Stuck!

How do I know when the devils using someone, anyone? Here's the clue… they were once happy and now they begin to complain about everything. They start participating in other ungodly conversations. They start having their mindset shifted from the things and the movement of God. Shifted to unhappy thoughts and pattern of defeat, because they are just stuck. Show me a complaining person, and I will show you a Non-Praying and Non-Atmosphere changing person. Yep! That's what you should look for, the person who is not changing and growing up in CHRIST. Flee from them and run to prayer, for they will soon melt like wax! It's a fact that even your car changes gears when it's driving. We must do the same in the Christian Faith. We must learn how to **GROW UP** and accept Godly and Spiritual changes which will lead to **POWER**.

Others Will Pass By A Car That is Stuck On The Highway of Life

Have others passed by you while you have been stuck in the time of non-movement and unpreparedness? Yes, they have! Why? It's because you refuse to be honest with yourself. Recognize that you are not growing in the grace of God in prayer and in relationship. Until now you may never have even invested in a prayer training book like this one, because you thought, "I know HOW to pray."

We Must Guide You To "Increase Your Rate of Answered Prayers"

Let me ask you something, what is the rate your prayers really get answered? Is that working for you? Well it's time to learn how to pray in FAITH, PUT GODS WORD to WORK FOR US, and We must "Lift up the Prayers" and take it to another level, go higher in God. In other words, **COME ALIVE!** Be excited to talk to God. Be excited to learn new prayer levels and decree them with POWER! Yes, Feel His power and embrace His Love.

You should do this every time you get on your knees. We need to enter in with the fervent of passion before God, a love before God that changes the atmosphere. If we are really honest with ourselves and our prayers, we would admit that very rarely are our prayers changing the atmosphere. But we can change this today with Prayers from the ALTAR, a Shepherds cry. Let this next 90 days put you on an awesome path of Prayer.

By the time you end the Year, you will be so much closer to God. Now you can really start a "Prayer circle" (5 people) dedicated like you to pray every day for 90 days and do these prayers 4 times a Year. Praying effective prayers to keep your family, yourself, Ministry, and lives covered under the Blood of Jesus! Get exciting people, or just do it by yourself knowing corporately others are praying with you as well, all over the Kingdom of God! So it is time to make your move, God is there to meet you with the Fire so let's get on FIRE!

Be the Same in "A Prayer Feverishness Attitude" All the Time!

I say to you all, if you have one standard prayer you do when you're in front of people and one standard prayer you do when you think people are at church, "and ole well this is what I'm going to do," attitude of prayer, worship or praise; then you're phony. You're a hypocrite and you're betraying God.

I sense that spirit of betrayal in a lot of you. (This is going to be meat for the grown folks.) You're really not praying! You're really not in warfare! You are just haphazardly saying words with no passion or no meaning! You are not moving God! That why He's not responding! Would you respond to a phony lover? The only time you're praying is if something is really wrong, and then you want to bombard Heaven. God is not that type of Lover! If the only time your prayer shifts is when people are watching you, then you're another person! You're not a prayer ambassador, and God wants a refund, because he brought you with a price, you are not your own.

We Must Guide You to "Kingdom Prayers and Language"

Your life has been purchased by demanding blood, the Blood of Jesus Christ, and he remains the same, FAITHFUL and 100% in. So he demands the same type of respect, love, and loyalty, at all times, at all cost. We are ministers of FIRE! So what if it's just you in prayer you should still light up the room like its ten thousand people watching you. Bring Gods fire to the ALTAR! And if you can't do that in prayer, then who are you really serving?

I just want to tell you, "It's not about me, it's not about you. It's about the Kingdom!" If it's only one of you, you should be praying like its ten thousand people. When people come up to you and come into your presence they should say "Oh my God, I can't wait to get in there. It's Fire!" So that "Betrayal Spirit" causes you to move away from God and into a "Religious Act" and slothful behavior must die! Why? Because when you should be with Jesus, you're off with the enemy being tricked, derailed, and making plans to sell out our Savior. Know where you choose to be, make the decisions of who you really are and what you're planning to do. **Take time to be with Jesus and you will not be able to be trapped by the enemy as much!**

The Kingdom has a language, and that language is Faith. Your prayers must speak faith. You must learn the words of Warfare, Intercession, Petition, Supplication, Favor, Grace, Declarations and Kingdom Power.

Prayer is a fact, we must pray! There is a correct way to pray. I hope this book will indeed guide you into Effective Prayer and a Successful Life of Abundance through prayer.

Chapter 2

Exposing the Spirit of Deception That Hinders Our True Prayer Life

NOTES

Chapter 2

Deception #1: Lying To Your Own Self

Now I want to give a word of wisdom and expose the **Spirit of Deception**. The great deception is to oneself. You can deceive yourself. You deceive yourself by saying that you are "okay" when you are not! When you're not even praying, and have no REAL time with God, you are not okay. You can deceive yourself into believing that you are righteous. You can deceive yourself into thinking that you are in line with God and that the things you do are "not wrong" before God. That it's okay NOT to pray. What a deception!

Deception #2: No Time For God

When you make prayer a **religion and not a relationship**, you have no time for God. I know I like it when Bishop Rice calls me "just to check in for a minute." It makes me smile to know he has me on his mind. As busy as he is, he took a break to say "honey I just called to say Hi and I love you." Yes, just like those quick check ins, they are powerful to help our relationship grow. You must have no excuses not to check in with God! Just to say "I Love You." That's relationship! And really that's the highest form of spiritual communication. But God wants a lot more. Check-ins should be routine, specific, and have time to receive instructions to lead our day. Not to lead ourselves, but be led by God. Just checking in for 5 minutes is fun for God and a blessing for you.

Really ask yourself, "Why don't I pray more if it's that simple?" Well maybe if I had some prayer guidance… in a book…

you will decree and communicate more with God. Amen! Well now you have the tools to produce routine communication that will cause you not to fall not trials so early. Remember the enemy will let you talk to everyone else but God, even him! The Enemy will come in and have you have a conversation with yourself, and his spirit of pride and deception, until you convince yourself you're okay. Americans do a lot of this.

The "Spirit of Deception" doesn't want you to move forward. The Spirit of Deception does not want you to understand that Gods mandate on your life is to consistently move you forward. So he'll say, "you're alright" when the Pastor comes by and tells you to lift your hands up, or lift your voice up higher in the prayer time. Your spiritual response should not be lazy and rebellious or questioning "why do I have to do that." It should be, "No, I'm NOT okay. I need to press more to touch the very heart of God."

We must ask ourselves am I really in tune with the spirit of the Living God? It's not how you shake, and show outward emotions, (but some of the emotions will come), but how you really, move the hand of God, is the result in your time with God, and a life of Altar Prayer. Your altar can be anywhere you create a time and a place to meet God, a place where you can meditate, journal, hear the voice of God, receive instructions, pray, praise, worship, listen, weep, and rejoice, without being disturbed! That's a mighty altar for prayer! Where ever you can create an undisturbed place and space where you can expect God to show up, it is your ALTAR. God will meet you were ever you purpose to meet him. He is so kind like that. If you call his name in worship and prayer he will answer you and show you mighty and great things.

Many people have shelves, mats, pillows, towels, blankets, prayer covers, candles, incents, rooms, special places, cars, work booths, bathrooms, and closets, in which they have created as a space to meet God (I prefer no bathrooms). I am sure God is saying, "SAY A WORD DAUGHTER! Tell them to get me out of the bathroom. That's not how I want to see them!" Where ever you can create a worship area to meet God, do so, so you can learn to command your destiny in the Power of God!

Deception #3: You Know It All About God

Ok... what you don't know CAN HURT YOU! A lack of proper day setting and a lack of evening declarations can HURT YOU! Can you command your day, your morning, your increase, and your blessings? Heaven wants to move, but can you move the hand of God? Thinking you know all there is to know about God is a true deception!

Self-deception is the worst kind of deception. We must cause someone else to be blessed, and not just move ourselves with our own emotions. True prayer time will cause you to come out of Self Deception and Self Religious activities. God said we have to deal with this.

There is a deceiving demon that is running through the church. This spirit will make you think, "I'm okay because God is speaking to me and using me." Is He really? Or is this a Spirit of Deception? The Bible instructs us to examine ourselves daily. So when was the last time you took the time to really look at yourself? To SEE if you be found in the faith! David said, "Oh wicked man am I." So we should do the same self-examination and say, "It's my fault, I need to do better. I am a ratchet person, I need to be delivered. God take it out of me." We must be honest and open to God and true to Him. This is not a popular message, but the prophetic church needs to hear this and receive it. It is the time for correction. Allow grace to enter your heart and let our Father correct us through the leaders that He has placed over our lives to perfect us, and the ministries He has sent us to reign in.

Deception #4: The Purpose of the Church

Where did you read in the word of God to "Come to the Church to FEEL GOOD?" The answer is **NOWHERE**! The church is a place for perfecting the saints. Just like a hospital is a place to find out what's wrong with you and get cured, so you can be better and go home! I have not read one scripture yet that says, "Go to the house of God and feel good." No, it says, "Rend your clothes and repent." Not just for yourself, but for your fore Fathers and for your children. It says, "Examine yourself." Look at yourself.

Deception #5: God Will Not Judge, Condemn and Correct Us

Change, transform, be cut between the bone and the marrow, weep, and put on the new man! Yes our God is a God of Love, but He is also a God that will move by His hand when we operate in the spirit of wickedness. It's not just "Old Testament," its Bible. This is the God we serve, Jehovah, an all consuming fire. The God that's just. The God that's fair. The God that avenges us. The God that puts up and the God that snatches down. And I know we want this tip top, Rudy too little God.

We serve an awesome, a mighty, a powerful, a back breaking, thunderstorm moving, earthquake shaking God, and His word fulfills that. He is a God of judgment. So we must expose "deception." When we are in the Spirit of Deception we have a lot of pitfalls. And those pitfalls can be eliminated when you use the role of the Holy Spirit to protect you.

When the Holy Spirit warns you of an approaching catastrophe then you know that you are in line with God.

Deception #6: The Purpose of the Holy Spirit/ Holy Ghost

Some of us have so much Holy Ghost, but never seem to be "warned about anything". The Holy Ghost will warn you trouble is coming. The Holy Ghost will show you something is wrong. The Holy Spirit will show you that "you need to go deeper in God" because I'm seeing you praying on the surface. The Holy Ghost will show you all things. The Holy Ghost will discern your hidden motives and unspoken agendas.

Allow the Holy Spirit to have its "Perfect Work" in you! If you get the wrong person in your life, that person can throw your whole destiny off by 20 years with one conversation. **A lie can devastate the noblest dream.** Many people have been lied on and because they couldn't bounce back they'd just quit their Journey. "Oh they lied on me. What they said about me wasn't true and now people believe it." They get thrown off their Journey. A trap can destroy a thousand dreams that God will have for you. One "bad investment" can make all your life savings disappear. The Holy Spirit is there to show you how to anticipate the diversities and adverse atmosphere that you'd enter into. But you have to know how to enter into the secret place of the Most High. You have to know how to stay in the presence of God. You have to long for His presence. You have to begin to journal all that God is doing and saying in your life.

Deception #7: All Days Are the Same

You have to see what times and seasons you operate in because just like the seasons that go and come (Summer, Spring, Winter, and Fall), "there's a season to everything" as mentioned in Ecclesiastes. There's a season when the enemy is coming to deceive you. There's a season that you must avoid prophesy's that are not sent by God, but are to distract you from your assignment.

There's a season to pray, pray, pray, worship, worship, worship, read, read, read, grow, grow, and grow!

Not every prophesy that sounds good is good for you. I remember when someone prophesied to me and said "Change the times you meet God." God didn't tell me that. Why would I change the times I'm meeting God when God is still meeting me there? I wouldn't change it unless God wasn't showing up! Now to some of you all would go change what God is telling you to do because you don't have spiritual discernment to know that the enemy sends word too. And the enemy will have you out of the covering and every prayer you're praying is null and have no power.

. **Deception #8: There Is No Enemy To Distract You**

The enemy did the same thing to Eve. He came and told her the opposite of what God said to distract her from the "True Word" of God! God will tell us "No, Don't, Not so," but because we don't like that word the enemy knows we are not really obedient in our hearts towards God and His direct instructions. He takes advantage of the feeble, weak, frail, disobedient and rebellious in Spirit. He takes advantage of those who do not know the force, character and relationship of the Father. He is seeking those that will accept instructions not of God. Know what your Father sounds like, know His voice! I just use that example because if he's bold enough to come to me, surely he's bold enough to come to you. He'll tell you to change this, do this and do that

Deception #9: Once A Week In Church Is Enough

That's why you have to have your ear attended to the word of God. That's why we provide here, at the Greater Harvest Christian Center Churches Worldwide-IGACCW, 3 to 4 life enrichment times a week for you to eat. Just like you can't survive on one meal for 7 days, you cannot survive spiritually just eating a half of cup of rice for 8 or 9 days. Sooner or later you're going to be in "Spiritual Famine." You're going to be weak. And when the enemy comes in like a flood you will have nothing in you to lift up a standard.

Ministry doors should be opened for service more than they are closed, not the opposite. Why have a place for Ministry for only 5 hours a week? The Temple should be open! Therefore we provide the meal, the spiritual meals, so you can maintain strength in the word of God. They sang a song from the word of God called "I have a hiding place, a shelter in God. I seek Him in the fat years, and in the lean times He still provides."

God says out of the mouth of "babes comes perfected praise." In other words, they don't have anything that's hindering them between the word that's being revealed and what's hidden in Spirit. The babies will receive and cry out Hallelujah, while the older members are sitting on the pews looking dead. You can have so much stuff in your Spirit that you have to shuffle all that to the side in order to get to that "free babe" praise. Hallelujah…

This will take more than 4 hours a week, two on Sunday and maybe Bible Study. No, No, No! You'll need more than that to service and be in God! I am a hungry babe, I need to eat often! I need my "Spiritual Food Fix" frequently. I cry to God to be filled in Him. I want to be with Him at least 5 times a week. I push myself for a "Relationship" with God. Relationships take time, energy, love, support and communication! I can't have a healthy relationship with anybody on just 2 hours a week. I need to be held, touched, communicated with, and so does God!

Deception #10: Bigger Churches Are Better Churches

We must not be distracted from worship service, Bible studies, and other Spiritual eating opportunities. **The demon comes to slay the sheep.** That demon didn't come for me, because he knows I'm going to still be standing. He came for you, because he figure if he can get you dislodged, up rooted and unfocused, you would leave your destiny and leave your assignment. He figured that if enough church members left, the Church would close down. The real plan of the devil is to shut down "true" churches and "true" prophetic and apostolic voices. He really isn't concerned with those that are lead by homosexuals, lesbians, liars and whoremongers. But if there's someone that's really leading from God, that's who he really wants to get you away from. He's not concerned with large buildings that are only opened 2 days a week, but he fights "Deliverance Ministries" and Churches that challenge you to change and grow! A fight will be on!

Deception #11: Flattering Words

Now let me show you how powerful this is. We have Friday Night Testimonies at my church and we've had people stand up and say, "This is the best church I've ever been in. I felt so much Love when I came into this church. These leaders can teach! I have to know how to stay in the presence of God. You have to long for His presence. You have to begin to journal all that God is doing and saying in your life.

Chapter 3
A Real Shepherds Job

NOTES

Chapter 3

As a shepherd, if you're the wolf, "I'm going to kill the wolf so that the sheep can live." It's that simple, it's my JOB! Well there are many things that can come to kill the lambs of God, the Sheep of The Kingdom, and I am assigned as a "True Shepherd" to kill them before they kill the sheep! I'm going to get rid of every form of distraction. I'm not going to let people burden me down unnecessarily. "I'm at a point that if you don't love me like I love me, then baby be gone." We don't even need to have a conference if this is not the church for you. If you're not growing and you can't see the benefits of being a member here, then you can leave. If your life is changing for the better and you want to go back to the pack, then go. That's the attitude of "A Real Kingdom Shepherd" Pastor must have. Any other attitude will eventually kill the sheep because wolves will form a pack in your pasture and destroy others while you sleep. It is okay when the wolves go so the sheep will grow.

Most people who leave the church say, "I have never been taught like this. This is the best teaching I've ever had." Yet they turn around and go back to the vomit that they left. Now that they're growing, they're shaking, they're moving, and going where they need to go they want to leave. Now they want to go back to the dirt like a pig in the parlor, to roll around in filth and mud. (That's what they wanted all the time) Even in the world, if you didn't want me, I didn't want you. There are a few you really can't help, and it's okay. Don't be deceived, you and I are not the savior. We are Shepherds, and must also protect our anointing as well as our spiritual lives.

Grumbling Spirit

We are in deception to believe that membership is not a collaboration. I don't want anybody to be a member at my Church that doesn't want to be! When I had a job, I've always worked very high positions. Vice President, CEO, Head of Human Resources, and so on. I didn't want anybody working for me that didn't want to be there. **You will always find employees that will grumble about their job.** They will talk about how bad the job is, but then they stay 20 years. "The foolish people" will allow them to get into their ears with all that mess and contaminate their spirit. And then they are so puffed up that when the supervisor says something to them, their attitude is bad. Here is a life lesson…You may end up getting fired or you can end up quitting, and "that person" is still there on the job. They will probably retire from that company they "hate" so much. So you were contaminated and loss behind someone with a spirit of deception that manifested as a "Grumbling Spirit, all to get you away from what they wanted. Wow!

It's the same way in the church, there's always going to be people that are disgruntled. That will sit around and murmur and complain about this and talk bad about that. I've learned to pass those people by, because I'm not going to let you contaminate me. Here is the truth, "I want to be my members Pastor." If they are true members, Praise the Lord! I want to shepherd them! If they are wolves then they must go, or die, for the safety of the sheep.

Most pastors, like myself, we want to Pastor you. So if anyone doesn't want to be a part of what God is doing in that house, there's a McDonalds down the street. We have a praying church, and I will not stop praying because someone thinks I'm praying too long. Your life can only be fixed by prayer. How many hours are given to TV? Take half that amount and use it to PRAYER and watch God work. The Church needs PRAYER, to hear and communicate with God. We have to stop acting DEAD and purpose our hearts to hear God.

If they want Burger King or McDonalds and we're fine dining, it's okay. There are so many Burger Kings around. Burger King serves millions of people that McDonalds doesn't. McDonalds serves people that Burger King doesn't serve. But I don't have a desire to stop being who I am to be the burger King "King" or have the "M" on my arches. What God has put in me is good for the feeding and healing of the nation. It is good for the sheep's that hear my voice and another they do not follow.

We have to come out from that Spirit of Deception, that deceiving devil. That devil that tells us as a Church that, "We do not need prayer, to not do too much praise and to cut the worship short." That same devil of deception is the same spirit that dealt even with Eve in the garden, it's that same spirit. One day you will be in leadership, and we'll see what you're going to do. Until then may I suggest to you that you sit and learn with a grateful spirit? Do not be deceived by the enemy. Learn to pray while you are waiting, take my word for it, you are going to need it! Learn with a grateful spirit, because you haven't paid the cost yet to walk in the shoes.

We Must Fix the Problem

What is the problem? **The problem is that you don't spend much real time with God,** and a large majority of those who say they do are phony, "Holy Actors." Somebody said something to me the other day about another "Women of God" and the way she did something at her ministry with her husband. I had to let them know, "Baby, wait a minute. You can't tell me about how the Women of God is supposed to act, because you have never been a Women of God. You haven't walked holy for one whole year. You can't lay a hand on a headache. And please don't quote me any scriptures you can't live by. Take those scriptures and use them for yourself and get your life straight." But most of us don't reply like this! I would like to propose a question... If you have so many scriptures and "Greater is He that is in you," and all this other wonderful stuff, then why aren't you improving? Fix your own life! And then go abroad. Until then, be a loyal, faithful and respectable member!

The word works, so it's something between you and the word that's not working. Now the word is working for me! Greater is He that is in me, because I understand how not to move in the Spirit of Deception. So greater is He that is in me... the Holy Ghost that exposes the Spirit of Deception that is in me. So greater is He that is in me. Greater! Greater is He that is in me! So I'm lead by the spirit, there is no condemnation. Because I am really recognizing, admitting and quitting the foolish example and fixing me!

It's when you stop being led by the Spirit that condemnation comes in. I'm no longer under condemnation because I'm not lying, I'm not gossiping, I don't back bite, and I'm not in your business. I have no sin that I'm participating in willfully over and over again. "I don't purpose to sin." I don't run from house to house being a busy body. I don't have other people in my business. Most time I mind my business and the telephone ring. And then I make an Apostolic decision of what needs to be done. Holiness, Righteousness, Grace and Favor are my mantel, and I Love so God can use me anywhere and anytime.

I try to be ready everyday and everyway. When I fly around for speaking engagements, there's no Gigolo waiting in my hotel room because I refuse to allow the enemy to deceive me. When you're talking, I'm praying. That's why I ask so many questions. While you were talking God gave me the questions to ask. And when I ask that question and get another answer then God says, "No that's not all." So I'll ask another question until we get to the real root of the matter. The part you didn't want me to know. You wanted me to go off what you were saying. But baby, I'm not in this to be deceived of what you want me to be. I'm in this because

God has anointed me. This is where we all have to be to be Kingdom Minded, and not deceived.

I am not the kind of person to that be skinning and grinning and laughing. I'm not "a silly woman lead captive by my own imagination." I don't put myself out on people. I try to live sin free as much as I possibly can. I'm not wicked, I'm not cheating on my husband and I'm not looking for another. I'm not watering down the gospel. I don't police my church. I don't come by their house to sneak and see what they're doing. No, you bring it to me. Then I'm going to expose it. We need to all grow from these things. And when you know whose Faith you're following, you need to follow that kind of Faith.

Sign #1: How To Identify Your Enemy

What's an enemy? **An enemy is anyone who weakens your influence with others.** That's why I say some of you all have been "enemies to the Church."

A few years ago, a person who used to be a member of my church and left said to a current member, "You should come over here to the church I'm at now?" And that person left as well. 6 months later, neither one of them attends church anymore. But this harm came from someone who said they loved me.

When you join a church it's just like a marriage, it's a covenant. Here's an earthly example. I have a husband and you are my best friend. Male and Female, follow me. My husband and I have come together and birthed some things. Now we're married with children. Then something happens and we split up, not divorced, but we just separated. Now you have another friend and you tell her you're going to introduce her to my husband. "Something is wrong with that, right"? That's wicked. That means that you were never for me. You always wanted to get your friend with my husband. Now that you think you have a little window of opportunity, you spread it out in the name of Jesus... and that's wicked! That's the devil tearing up the Church house. You're causing confusion, and you don't like me. You knew I was going to pray for reconciliation. But you step in and caused permanent damage because you were loss!

If I know your Pastor, and I know your pastor is preaching the word, why would I tell you to leave your church and come over here where I am? I'm not going to tell you to come to my church. I'm not going to tell the name of my church because I love that Pastor and I will do them no harm. That's the right way to do it. I don't go there anymore. But you're married to this church. So you should never want to take anybody from this church. That's the devil and all his friends, that's the spirit of deception.

Sign #2: An Enemy Is Not a Friend, It's A Wolf. And A Wolf Will Kill A Sheep

The enemy is someone that wants to weaken the influence of others. At the first sign a shepherd has turned his back, the wolf will attack. It's always looking for every opportunity. So anybody that would weaken your influence with others is an enemy. If you have a friend on your job who is always saying something bad about you, that's not your friend. "When you're on a job, you're sent on a Kingdom Assignment." You should be winning souls into the Kingdom and inviting them to a worship experience with you. Truth is, only one in every 50,000 working relationships will remain friends after one person leaves the job. 1 in every 50,000! So then that's not your friend, that's an associate. "You're sharing space and time because of an assignment in your life." So don't get it twisted about who your friends are. Keep your true kingdom assignment in mind.

Sign #3: An Enemy Is Anyone Who Focuses On Your Past Instead Of Your Future

If you did drugs ten years ago and God saved you and you're a missionary now, the enemy comes and says, "You're just a dope head. That's all you'll ever be. I don't care what those people at the church say about you. They don't know you like I know you." And the enemy is right, they know you a little better, because the "you" the enemy thought he knew died. This person that's living he knows nothing about. And because he doesn't know you, he doesn't know your future. The enemy doesn't know what God has said about you. The little interim time in your life when the enemy was working was increasing your testimony. And when you're working on your testimony, those things that you did then, you no longer will do. Hallelujah! Glory to God! I was working on my testimony. The enemy can only talk about your past, and the past people they knew, all to try and keep your reflection on yesterday. That is not your today or your tomorrow. So laugh! Satan is playing an outdated song that you don't sing anymore. It was something that can bring others to the point that they can say, "If God can bring you out of this then He can deliver me out of that."

That's why I can tell you all, when we come to church were going to praise Him. Because **when I went to the club I gave the Devil all my praise.** I didn't care how stupid the dance looked we did it anyway, and we did it in front of an audience. We did it until we were drenched in sweat, and most of the time there wasn't any seats to sit in. It's what we call the "hole in the wall" club. I know you all are use to the big lavish clubs, where everybody has the Grey goose and the big round white tables. Where did I learn about Grey goose? Some of my members (that were my members) had a party and other people were drinking grey goose and are supposed to be saved. When we were younger we had Crown Royal, Rum and Coke, and Vodka and Sprite. The poor people had Boone's Farm, Johnny Walker Red, 20/20, and a couple of those other drinks. And when you got a little of what we called "white lighting" in you, everything loosens up. Moves that you didn't think you could do, you came out with. You all think I dance now, owe wee. Okay, yesterday's story. I am saved and I know it! I'm just letting you know God can save you from the inside out.

Blessed be the rock of my salvation. You don't know tight clothes! I won the tight jeans contest quite frequently and with the same pair of tight white jeans! You all don't understand! So when God saved me, no one had to tell me my clothes were too tight. Nobody had to tell me to put on underwear. **The Holy Ghost told me.** Nobody had to tell me stuff was inappropriate because when I went to put it on, stuff just started happening. I would say, "God is this okay?" And I would hear God say, don't wear that. I had chains, diamonds and rings and gold. I went to put it on my neck and God said give every bit of that away. I said what? Hold on, wait a minute, I need another sign. I have to know that's Jesus (And He didn't say pawn it and get some money for it). He said give it away. Give it away! That was like 5 pay checks! He said yeah, **now what you did for the devil do it for the Kingdom.**

That's why I don't have a problem giving. God will bring you out of the "Spirit of Deception," if you want to be free. Because whatever you did for "the devil," when God saves you, you're supposed to do more for God. Some of you act like you haven't done anything for Satan, just so innocent. You might've not been caught, but you did something. I had a lady one time who was talking bad about somebody with 5 kids out of wedlock. I said you would've had more than that if you had been able to produce; because you were with every man on the block. Sometimes people will want to make you feel bad about stuff you've been caught in, and they did the same things, but didn't get caught. Truth be told, if half of us would have been caught we would be in jail today. **Thank God for grace and mercy.**

So when the enemy comes to you all slick and sliding; you don't need to stick your head in the sand like you haven't done anything. Like you never saw the devil before or never heard a slick rap line. You don't need to act as though you've been saved all your life. Like you don't understand this is a lie from the pits of Hell, a spirit from which it comes out of. You need to boldly stand-up (where no man has gone before) into the presence of that enemy and say, "You're the spirit of distraction. You're the spirit of deception. I will have no parts of this."

Sign #4: An Enemy Is Anyone Who Attempts To Weaken Your Passion

He weakens your passion through "Content and Criticism." They are trying to weaken your passion because they're your enemy. When I went to the club 5 nights a week, no one ask me why are you going to the club. There's people in the bingo house 5 nights a week and nobody ask why they are there spending their money. There are people at the moon shine house and there's nobody asking why they are there. There are people that gamble all night long, and no one at the casino asks them why they are there every night. But now that I'm in the church and choose to come 3 and 4 nights a week, now people are concerned about where I am spending my money. **Now that I'm doing something positive, people want to know where I am spending my time.** But when I was doing something negative you weren't concern. And that's where I have a problem!

It's the Spirit of Deception that comes to deceive me into believing that you care about me. But when I had my skirt up to my navel and showing my body to everyone in the streets, you should have told me "put on some clothes on." **Now that I have some clothes on you want to call me "old" because I have respect for myself.** Now that prayer is working in my life! Now that I look like I got some Holy Ghost! "Now that I have some good sense and no longer look like a stripper, hooker or a pole dancer you're concerned. People want to try to condemn you, to criticize you and try to bring you down to their level. I've been at that level before and all I got was a whole lot of nothing, but now I am defeating the devil. I'm not going to let my enemy take me back, NO WAY!

This is what you must be prepared to face when Prayer becomes active in your life. **People will turn on you and try to make you feel bad for changing for the better.** Somebody, anybody, everybody should know that the enemy is going to criticize you when you finally get it together. When you finally get a job they try and make you miss work. "That's the devil." When you start going back to school, all before they kept your kids for free. But start trying to do something positive, they want to charge you. Don't act like you never met the devil before. I know it might be your family members or your friends. I understand you don't want to "bust" them out! But when it's all about the Kingdom, you have to rage war against the devil.

His "disciples are called demons and devils" and Christ's disciples are called Saints. The more you praise God, the more you step on the devils head. The more you step on the devil's head, the more he wants to rise up. You'll push him down on one side and if you're not very careful he'll stomp you down on the other side. Beat that devil like the mole coming out of the machine. Stomp him until his head hurts. Until he has to go lay down and fall asleep. Stomp him until he can't find another hole to come up out of. Greater is the anointing that's really in you.

Sign #5: An Enemy Of Distraction Is Anyone (Even Your Own Self) Who Thinks You Are Unworthy Of Achieving A God Given Goal

Sometimes the enemy can be YOU. Sometimes God will say you are a missionary and you don't believe in what God is saying. God will call you to be a Pastor, and you'll tell God why you can't do it. God will tell you to step up and be a church mother and you go and act crazy like you never act crazy before. God will tell you to start teaching children's church then all of a sudden you'll start being late coming in. God will call you on the praise team then you'll start putting everything before rehearsal. **You are so prone to "Self-Destructive" behavior to the point that you destroy even what God has said concerning your future.** And yes, something else is going to say, "Girl you know you're not a Missionary. You know you want to hit this blunt (weed, gunga)." That's the devil! Run to your prayer temple and fall on the altar and ask for strength!

Sign #6: Your Enemy Is Someone Who Knowingly Distracts You From Moving Upward In God

The bible tells me that what's on the inside will show up on the outside. So if I am who I say I am on the inside, then it should show up on the outside. It doesn't matter if I'm in the church doors, Kmart, or wherever, I should be the same. No one should ever say, "What! You're the missionary?" It all has to line up. If prayer is not changing you, you will lose your Spiritual Promotion!

You are designed to be promoted. Ask yourself, do I pray enough to be promoted? Am I preventing myself from moving upward? It's not your leadership that's holding you back, it's you. We promote the faithful. You can't say you want to be promoted by God and half the time you're here and the other half you're late.

You come in with all kinds of bad spirits. Somebody has to pump you up! Then you're not ready for leadership. When you hit the parking lot or the street you should say, "I was glad when they said let us come to the house of the Lord."

Purpose To Spend Time In God's House (Extra Extra Time)

When you come in greet your leader. Ask the question, "Is there anything you may have for me to do, if not I'm going to the altar to pray." You have to stop being distracted. You have to stop going backwards and go forward. A lot of times you are not going forward in God because you are always late. **LATE PEOPLE ARE NOT PRAYING PEOPLE ... GOD WOULD NOT HAVE YOU LATE ALL THE TIME.** You're late in the morning and you're late at night. You're late for what you want to be late for. But you're on time for what you are on time for. Doctor offices say be on time for your appointment. Your job tells you to be to work on time. The Church says come... but your deceived and come late! Stop playing with yourself, that's the demon of deception and distraction, the spirits that keeps you from pressing into the move of God. The Saints are too distracted! **Distractions will keep you delayed and denied.** You should not let everything distract you. You know it's going to take an hour and a half to get to church, so you'll leave an hour late. But yet you say "I am ready to lead, to be a Pastor to somebody." Really! Well let's work on defeating the little things that spoil our success, in Prayer and Actions.

Chapter 4
Overcoming Being Deceived By Staying In Prayer

NOTES

Chapter 4

What are we talking about? The Spirit of deception! It is the spiritual realm that will lull us to sleep and cause us NOT to want to be in Prayer. It will keep us un-alert to the tricks of the enemy, and it will try to deceive us so that we are unable to defeat the enemy before he has a chance to come to our door unaware. Let's continue to look at 1 Kings 14.

> *⁶And it was so, when Ahijah heard the sound of her feet, as she came in at the door, that he said, Come in, thou wife of Jeroboam; why feignest thou thyself to be another? for I am sent to thee with heavy tidings.*

> *"Go, tell Jeroboam, Thus saith the LORD God of Israel, Forasmuch as I exalted thee from among the people, and made thee prince over my people Israel, ⁸And rent the kingdom away from the house of David, and gave it thee: and yet thou hast not been as my servant David, who kept my commandments, and who followed me with all his heart, to do that only which was right in mine eyes ;⁹ But hast done evil above all that were before thee: for thou hast gone and made thee other gods, and molten images, to provoke me to anger , and hast cast me behind thy back:*
> *Therefore, behold, I will bring evil upon the house of Jeroboam,*

Wait a minute, God is saying this? So now if you say, "God will not bring evil on anybody," then the devil has deceived you.

You are acting like the devil's own; you are a "lying wonder." You're in the spirit of deception. God will bring evil on you. If you are evil God will bring that same evil back on you. Is that in your bible? I did not make that up. Many will say, "How are we going to be a people of God talking about God is going to get me." The answer is because it's in my bible. I am a vessel of God, a mouth piece of his word, a TRUE PROPHET!

Most of you all must learn how to be a mouth piece of God, a true prophet or vessel of God, because you've never been one. You are in training to learn what you ought to be. You should know the bible, read it or put it in constant action for a lifetime or a FULL season. Keep living and growing and you will have lived longer as a saint then as a sinner, and then you will know what I mean! **EXPERIENCE TALKS!** Real experience, knowing GOD is the only way you can tell me what my God will do. Not just book knowledge, but faithful relationship is the next level in God. God shares special things, insights, truths and revealed glory to those whom become expecters of his visitations (friends). It's a beautiful life to live in and see the manifestations of Yahweh!

A Little Personal Testimony on Time Management

You can't be ready to lead somebody until you are ready to be in front of them. I worked at a job where I was the manager of over 800 apartment complex and we had church 5 nights per week. I didn't get off until about 6pm. So the first thing I did was to take only a 30 minute lunch break so I could get off 30 minutes early. I took my church clothes to work with me. I had good personal hygiene that I didn't have to run home and take a bath before coming to church. But the spirit of distraction can cause us to make a lot of excuses. We'll get dressed and go everywhere else we want to go. You will jump straight out of the bed and go to the grocery store. Throw on this and throw on that and run 3 fingers in your hair and be OUT of the house and gone. But when it's time to go to church you have to go home and take a 2 hour bath.

I had 3 children all raised in the church. I kept clothes in the trunk with wipes. I use to pick them up, wipe them off, put their clothes on, put them in the car and head to church. I went to work dressed for church because I was always anticipating the move of God that morning. So I definitely wasn't going to let anything or anyone distract me. I drove people to church, but they had to be on time and early, because I didn't want to be LATE!

I didn't have a lot of excuse over and over again. That's why I believe God promoted me. **So many people want to be promoted but they have so many excuses over and over again.** God does not promote people that make a lot of excuses. Week after week and day after day, no you need to be here. Make provisions for what you want God to make provisions for you with. You want God to move on time for you then be on time for God. You say you serve an on time God then why are you late? That means that you're not serving God. The demon of disillusion wants to hold you back and wants to pull you down. The demon of deception is saying to you, "It's alright I get there when you get there." It's a deceiving spirit. God doesn't honor halfway. And if you're working for your pay from God, then you've been docked so many times it isn't funny.

1 Kings 14: The Spirit of Deception

> *1 At that time Abijah the son of Jeroboam fell sick. ² And Jeroboam said to his wife, Arise, I pray thee, and disguise thyself, that thou be not known to be the wife of Jeroboam; and get thee to Shiloh: behold, there is Ahijah the prophet, which told me that I should be king over this people. ³ And take with thee ten loaves, and cracknels, and a cruse of honey, and go to him: he shall tell thee what shall become of the child.*

We must revisit this passage to expose the spirit of deception. He believed the prophet to be a righteous Prophet. See we all believe the prophet for what we want to believe the prophet for. You all believe the prophet to be righteous when you want them to be righteous.

To Be a Prophet You Have To Have a Prophetic Understanding

⁴And Jeroboam's wife did so, and arose, and went to Shiloh, and came to the house of Ahijah. But Ahijah could not see; for his eyes were set by reason of his age.

So I wanted to see how old he was, so I looked in chapter 11 verse 29. As you look backwards and forwards in the word, you begin to see things come in to play. (Now this same prophet that he saw back there is the same prophet he is sending his wife to now.) The Lord says to the prophet.... You see a true prophet will see what God wants to show us. **I don't have to see everything. But I will see the right things, Gods things.** God speaks to me. The Lord said to the prophet, "Behold the wife of Jeroboam will come unto thee because the son is sick." Now this woman has disguised herself trying to be somebody else (as instructed to by the King). The King that knew this man was a true man of God. People will come with that spirit of deception, trying to deceive you. Trying to prove who the prophet is. And when you're a real prophet of God, believe He will not let you be deceived. We work for God, we don't work for you. **God is not going to have us deceive by your foolishness.**

⁵And the LORD said unto Ahijah, Behold, the wife of Jeroboam cometh to ask a thing of thee for her son; for he is sick: thus and thus shalt thou say unto her: for it shall be, when she cometh in, that she shall feign herself to be another woman.

Had he not been prayed up he would've been deceived. That's why I said the problem is that we all are not praying. Now you see where I'm at in the beginning. **It's when you're not prayed up and don't have a relationship with God you get deceived.** You are still stuck on that same old prayer and God is not exposing anything to you, you need to come on up to another level. So you can see who people really are. This blind man can see and you all have two eyes and still can't see. You can't see the people who are opposing with their mouth, slick with their conversations, and slick with their attitudes. You can't see! **If you can't see you, then you need to change because God is exposing you and saying that you need some time in REAL PRAYER!**

God Is Not Going To Let You Be Hid From the TRUE Prophet

When you want to be real you will seek realness. God is not going to let you be hid from the real prophet. That's why a lot of people want to come Greater Harvest Christian Center, or to a true PROPHETIC CHURCH. And it's okay, because they want to come in contact with the real prophet. They've jumped and played around and had people say, "Oh God is going to bless you. God's going to do this and do that for you." But a real prophet may just say something like, "You need to stop gossiping and go fast and pray to get that demon out of your life." And yes, right in the middle of the prayer line. A true prophet may call you out and tell you what GOD needs for you to know. True people do want true prophetic people, so people come from all over the nation to get true insight for their lives!

A Prophetic Nation Should Train Their Eyes To See!

A prophetic nation shall rise up and see. The Prophet said, "Come on in" because he knew who she was before she got there. (Didn't I tell you all we can see you before you get here?) God has showed us most of you all before you came in the door. And he's shown me the next crop that's coming in. The true seekers are coming, let's get ready! Don't be blind, God needs seers because all are blind because you're not praying. Hallelujah! **You have to see these spirits coming, and know that they're coming for you.** That's why churches call me, because I can see. I can see the powers of darkness coming for you. You have to pray against these powers of darkness that oppose your destiny. You see there's a "lying deceptive spirit" going around saying, "God doesn't judge you." We must cancel this assignment of untruth. **Deception is raging against the church, causing everything to be in Gods house and Presence!** We true prophets must release truth and power in our lives to rise up and prophesy against deception.

I want you to see it in the bible that the prophet has authority. Everybody is not the same in the church. Don't let the devil deceive you. People may say, "I have just as much Holy Ghost as you have." No, you don't because God didn't call you into this office. God does not have you watching over anybody's soul. You can't even keep your own soul straight. Hallelujah! That's not being nasty, that's to know who you are in Christ. God said He called some. **"He CALLED SOME" but He didn't call all! Then of those who are called, FEW ARE CHOSEN.** Doesn't that sound like a difference? It does to me! Hallelujah! When it's your time to be called (that's when you have yourself together) that's when you should go and do greats works. Not before and destroy the lives of others while you practice with your" immature faith." Prophets must tell people to "wait" on their calling. Be ready to be disliked, but be ready to walk tall, and carry a Big Stick. God will sustain you, if you are real for Him.

God is not sending out any more "half-done baked bread. **All this bread that God is sending in this prophetic season out has to be all the way done!** How do you know? The people are getting matured in the faith of the word, and are not receiving "half-done prophets" and their foolishness. Now if you want "gooey half-done raw bread," then the matured ministry is probably not the place for you. You just need a little more Jesus and a lot more entertainment for your sweet milk taste buds. But when you cook meat and bread together... you stick the knife in it to make sure it comes out clean (a real cook knows what I mean). When I stick a knife in it and there's no gooey stuff on it, I know it's finally ready to come out the oven and be served.

True Shepherds Making Intercession, Must Be Foremost

I've read the bible backwards and forwards and I'm still learning and having things revealed to me daily. People who have never read the bible one time are trying to tell us about God. He said, "I will bring evil upon your house," this is the King's house. So if God will bring evil upon the King, what do you think he'll do to you? **"God will throw poop in your face if you disrespect his leaders and act up with the people of God."** Now the next time you go to have a conversation about your leadership, next time you think about hearing reproach on your Kingdom family, be careful.... You don't know whose ears God's prophet has tuned in to.

A true leader can be right there in the midst of your conversation, hearing you and not even be with you. They are the ones that have to pray and say to God, "Don't kill them, they're just foolish." Making intercession for you is what your leader does. By right God is suppose to crumble everything that comes our way because He's already told you not to "touch the anointed and do the prophets no harm." The scriptures quote, "Him that dieth of Jeroboam in the city shall the dogs eat; and him that doeth in the fields shall the fowls eat: for the Lord hath spoken."

He's telling this to the women. Most of you righteous religious self-appointed prophets would say, "I rebuke that in the name of Jesus." However, beware **you don't have any true power, when the "True Prophet" speaks.** The blood does not cover wickedness or evil doings. If you are not right by God the blood will not cover you in your sins and at some point God will judge your actions. The "True Church" must know this and Reverence God, Prayer, and Leadership. The Kingdom Authority of God, His Constitution and Lordship must be applied to our lives.

Let's look at 1 Kings 14:14-15

Shepherds must go back to Intercessory Prayer! Stop trying to use all these scriptures to defend your folly because they're not working for you. They're going to work against you and they're going to make you stand accountable even more than you were before. And God is going to say, "Oh, since you know the scriptures (him that knows to do right and doesn't do right) they shall be whipped with many stripes." And so the "dogs are going to eat you." Verse 12 says, *"Arise and get thee to thine own house, and when thy feet enter into the city, the child shall die."*

Watch Your Feet: 1 Kings 14:12

Don't let the deceiver bring you to your own death! Because that the job of the deceiver and that why we have to expose the deceiver; because he comes to bring you to death. Your mouth create atmosphere that somebody has to pay a price for. A defiled nasty attitude towards your leadership. Your attempts to come and deceive the prophets of truth vex the leaderships of God and will never come to any good. You come against the true prophet of God, the true women or man of God, it will always cause death to come to your house.

1 Kings 14:16

Don't let the deceiver, don't let any devil or demon come your way and cause you to miss your blessings. Please don't get in agreement with anything that doesn't line up with God's word. *"And he shall give Israel up because of the sins of Jeroboam, who did sin, and who made Israel to sin."*

Watch Who You Cleave To

You see that? Don't let anybody cause you to sin. *"...and Jeroboam's wife arose, and departed."* (1 Kings14:17) You see this is the prophet talking. The prophet still has power to bless and to curse according to the word of God. So do not say in your heart, "Oh I don't believe that!" I remember I had a member who was struggling with whether to pay her tithes and offering. I told her you're going to be cursed with a curse. She said, "Oh that doesn't apply to me Apostle, the blood of Jesus..." I replied, "Oh yes it does! This word applies to you just like it applies to everybody else." Malachi says, "Shall a man rob God?" You're going to be cursed with a curse! And the Bible is not going to change for you and it's not going to change for me. You're going to be cursed with a curse. She walked off from me, very hatefully. 3 days later she had a car wreck, not hurt, Praise God. Come to find out she had no car insurance.

Rebellion Can Lead You Further Than You Can Stand To Travel

For 3 years God kept her walking and catching the bus. She lost her car, all the money she spent going out with other people she could've just paid her tithes and offerings. See, God will show you He's God! God will show you whose boss. You can say what you want to, pop your neck, and quote your scriptures, but my friend....Those scriptures will cause more havoc on your life then you know what to do with. When the prophet speaks, listen and obey with the right spirit. Now she is a faithful tither and God has restored her. But she paid a price.

1 Kings 14:17-18

[17] And Jeroboam's wife arose, and departed, and came to Tirzah: and when she came to the threshold of the door, the child died;

[18] And they buried him; and all Israel mourned for him, according to the word of the LORD, which he spake by the hand of his servant Ahijah the prophet.

I want to tell you tonight, as we expose that spirit of deception, don't you be deceived by the Devil. Whether it's you or your crew, your four and no more, it doesn't matter. God's word is going to stand and let God's word be true and every man be a liar. I just wanted to share that with you in this chapter because I know it would be a blessing you. I want you to have the power to receive this word and not to be deceived by the "spirit of deception." I refuse it, I rebuke it, and I send it back to the pits! It only comes to delay and deny your destiny.

Let's review: 1 Kings 14:31 / 15:8 whether we are Kings or Priest, we must all give a final account to God! And I want the Kingdom of God to be READY.

God is looking for someone to come forth IN RIGHTEOUSNESS for Him. In your lineage there is someone destined to be righteous. Is that you?

Finally let's review 1 Kings 15:11-14. Ahijah did what was right in the sight of God. Can God count on you to do what is right in His sight?

Prayer will bring you to do what is right with God. Take your Prayer life and let it cause you to produce what is right in the sight of God. Our Father is depending on you to break every generational curse and become empowered to do what is right in His sight.

Know these 7 facts about prayer:

- Prayer Makes the Difference
- Prayer Makes the Hand of God Move
- Prayer Makes Our Hearts Pure
- Prayer Makes Us Different
- Prayer Makes Us Powerful
- Prayer Makes Us Precious
- Prayer Makes Us Children of God!

Chapter 5
Developing A Hiding Place

NOTES

Chapter 5

When I was a little I used to play a game call Marco-Polo, and one would say Marco and the other would say Polo. And you would have to have your eyes closed, and say "Marco," (and most people would be out of reach). Most of the time this game was played in the water. And you will try to find them with your eyes closed. They will say "Polo" to guide you to where they were all while doing things to try to distract you from finding them. Marco-Polo was a type of Hide and Seek.

Then we played a thing called Hide-And-Go-Seek. Young children now say Hiding-Seek. But we use to say Hide-And-Go-Seek, because somebody will hide and somebody will go seek. And if you hid in a good enough hiding place, they couldn't find you! If you hide in a good enough hiding place, you could not be discovered until you could get back around and hit the home base, and that person will be out and you will win the game. God begin to tell me, sometimes we as saints have to learn that God is our hiding place. He is a good enough hiding place that even when the wind blows (that means problems) real hard and the breaker dash (that means over shoot the shore line and go into other territories pass the shore line) Even when troubles are hitting you from everywhere, one behind the other, or all at one time. But God said I will hide you in the midst of all your trouble (Psalms 63:6).

For this "that shall everyone that is godly pray unto thee in a time when thou may be found." So there shall be a time when you may be found surely in the great floods of water, don't worry, but they shall not come nigh unto thee (Psalms 63:7).For thou are my hiding place. Thou shall preserve me from trouble. Thou shall compass about me with songs of deliverance. That means God wants to surround you at a time you may be going through something. He wants to surround us with songs of deliverance, breakthrough songs, songs that will help us come out of whatever situations that we might be in. That's why everybody that love God ought to have a song! You ought to have a song if it just but a 3 word song. You ought to have a song if you can't keep the beat. You ought to have a song if don't nobody want to hear you sing it. Everybody ought to have a song, because as you keep that song in your heart you develop a shield around you that keep the devil from your door. And a song ought to talk about the goodness of God.

There are three things the song ought to bring to you. First of all it ought to bring "Hope." I sing, "My hope is built on Jesus and His Righteousness." Why do I sing that? Because when folks are breaking my heart it lets me know that my "hope is in Jesus and not in the people." The song has to bring "Hope." It has to let you know that in Him you "live, and Hope, and have your being!" For thou "Oh Lord, are a shield and a fortress for me." Hallelujah you destroy my enemies. Let me not be ashamed. Let not my enemies triumph over me. Unto thee Oh Lord do I lift up my soul? You got to have a song! Hallelujah for the Lord is my Light and my Salvation, whom shall I fear? When they say you won't have a job, or when FPL start talking evil you say, "Whom shall I fear? For the Lord is my Light and my Salvation!" And when you get discourage you say, "Wait on the Lord and be of good courage." You got to encourage yourself and He will strengthen your heart! Hallelujah! You have to have a song. The song has to bring "hope."

Secondly, the song has to let you know that "God is in Control." It has to let you know where your position is. It has to let you know what your focus is, and where Gods position is. You have to have a song. When you learn to put a "song around you," it will put a "shield around you." The enemy won't be able to get to your heart because you will have a song. The Bible says, "Thou are my hiding place. Thou shall preserve me." That means He will put you in His jar. He will preserve you when they thought you would have spoiled. You will be preserve. You will bounce back and you will come back saying, "Jesus can work it out! Jesus can work it out!" He said that He will shield me with the "song of deliverance."

"I will instruct thee and teach thee my ways, which you shall go and I will guide you with my eye." Be not as the "horse or the mule which has no understanding." Don't be stubborn and rebellious. When something happens, you must sing you a song ! And at different points in your life that same song will mean different things to you.

At different points in your life that song will mean great things. Overcoming sorrow, victory, Praise and Worship! It will take you through grief. It will take you through heart ache. It will take you through promotion. It will take you through lonely spells. Hallelujah, God songs will take you through! When I get discourage I sing this song: "I'm satisfied, oh bless His name. He rescue me from sin and from shame, now my worries are over and my doubting has pass, and I thank God I'm satisfied at last!" I make myself satisfied. You create a wall of protection with your song.

The last thing that a song will do for you is will keep you Saved. It will keep you "Holy." When you sing about His Holiness it will keep you drawn. When you sing hymns it will keep you humbled. When you get a song focused on Jesus, it will take your mind off the problem! You must create your mouth to praise God! You can't sing "Amazing Grace how sweet the sound," and "Do it to me Baby" at the same time. You can't do it, that doesn't go together! Just like songs in the world create action (unholy fleshly action) for you, the songs of Glory will create action (holy, power moving, full of hope action) for you. Hallelujah!

Just like songs in the World perverts you (take your mind off God), the songs of Glory will keep you (and your spirit in perfect peace). That's why He says get a song so I can put a shield around! God what are you shielding me from? The world! Hallelujah! Songs of God shield you from sin, from backsliding, from thinking about the enemy and what He doing, from thinking about your personal problem, from thinking about oppression, depression, possession? God will become your hiding place. Have a song in your heart as you approach God in praise. If you want to know how to create a hiding place, you got to know how to create a song. You got to create a worship song. This will help you go higher in prayer.

Section 1
Prayers of Affirmation and Declaration

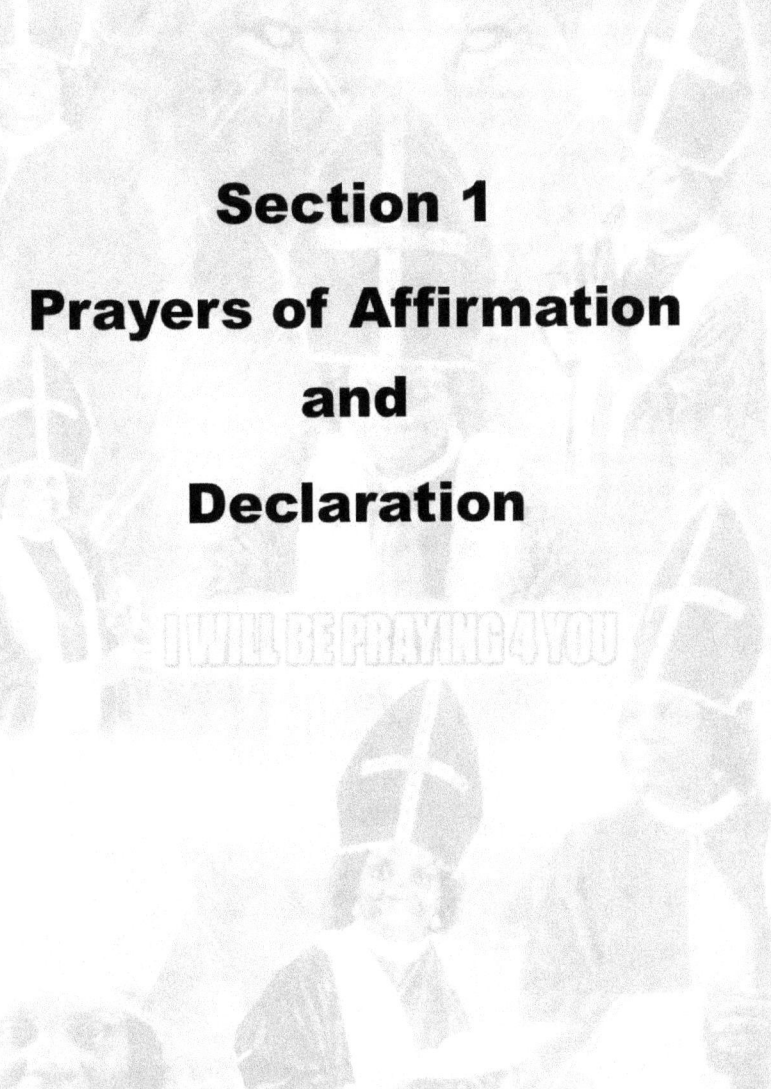

Section 1

Prayers of Affirmation and Declaration

A Christians Belief	Page 69
My Morning Declarations	Page 70
Who I Am In Christ	Page 72
I Am A Child of God	Page 73
Affirming The Grace of God To Me	Page 75
Affirming The Promises of God	Page 76
Prayer For The Church and It's Vision	Page 77
My Declaration of Victory and Faith for Daily Living	Page 80
Affirmations For My Spiritual Leaders	Page 81
Decree For Growth In Christian Vision	Page 83
Decree Of God's Love For Me	Page 84
Decree of Establishment	Page 85
Affirmations of Great Success	Page 87

NOTES

A Christian's Belief

I decree and believe in the Father Almighty, Creator of Heaven and Earth.

I believe in Jesus Christ, God's only Son, our Lord.

Who was conceived by the Holy Spirit.

Born of the Virgin Mary.

Suffered under the Pontus Pilate.

Was crucified dead and buried.

He aroused on the third day.

He ascended into Heaven.

He's seated now at the right hand of the Father.

He will come to judge the living and the dead.

I believe in the Holy Spirit.

The church world-wide.

The Communion of the Saints.

The forgiveness of sins.

The resurrection of the body and the life everlasting.

Amen

My Morning Declarations

I decree for myself, my leaders and my ministry, as I command my day.

I am in the Anointed One and his Anointing.

I am God's child, for I am born again of the incorruptible seed of the word of God.

I am forgiven of all my sins.

I'm washed in the blood.

I am a new creature in Christ.

I am the temple of the Holy Spirit.

I am delivered from the power of darkness and translated into the kingdom of God.

I am redeemed from the curse of the law of sin and death.

I am blessed.

I am a saint.

I decree I am the head and not the tail.

I am above and not beneath.

I am holy and without blame before him in love.

I am the elect of God.

I am established to the end,

make near to me my Heaven Father by the Blood of Christ.

I am set free.

I am strong in the Lord.

I am to dead to sin.

I am more than a conquer.

I am a joint-heir with Christ.

I am sealed with the Holy Spirit of promise.

My leader and I are in Christ by His doing.

I am accepted in the beloved.

I am complete in Him.

We are crucified with Christ.

I am alive with Him.

I am free from condemnation this day, in Jesus name.

As I set my day to line up with this word, bless my leaders, my church,

And my day as it is now directed by you father.

In the mighty name of Jesus.

I acknowledge you in all my ways and you will direct my path.

In Jesus name.

Amen

Chief Apostle Dr. J. G. Rice

Who I Am In Christ

I am blessed to be a blessing.

I am a member of the body of Christ.

I am reconciled to God by Christ.

I am qualified to share in His inheritance.

I am up-rooted and established in Christ and overflowing with thanksgiving.

I am born of God and the evil one does not touch me.

I am his faithful follower.

I am a fellow citizen with the saints of the household of God.

I am build upon the foundation of the Apostle's and Prophet's,

Jesus himself being the Chief Corner-Stone

I am overtaking with blessings.

I am His disciple because I have love for others.

I am the light of this World.

I am the salt of this Earth.

I am the righteousness of God. I am a partaker of His divine nature.

I decree and declare I am called of God.

I am an Ambassador for Christ.

I am God's workmanship created in Christ Jesus for God's works.

I am the apple of my Father's eye, healed by the stripes of Jesus.

I am being changed into His imagine.

In Jesus name.

Amen

I Am A Child of God

I confess I am a child of God.

I am a Christian.

I am chosen and appointed by Christ to bear His fruit.

I'm a slaved of righteousness and I'm enslaved of God.

I'm a son and a daughter of God and His temple dwells in me.

I decree I am joined to the Lord.

I am one with Him.

I am reconciled to God and I am a minister of reconciliation.

I am one with Christ.

I am an heir of God since I am a son and daughter of God after righteousness and holiness.

I am seated in Heavenly places with Him right NOW!!

I confess I am an expression of Christ because He is my life.

I am a chosen and dearly loved by God.

A am a son and daughter of light and not darkness.

A holy one.

A partaker of a heavenly calling.

One of God's lively stones.

I'm being brought up as a spiritual house.

I am a chosen race.

I am a royal priest-hood.

A holy nation.

A people up for God's own possession to proclaim the excellence of Him.

confess I am an alien and a stranger in this world that I temporarily live in.

I am an enemy to the devil.

I am "NOW" a child of God.

I am not the Great I AM, but the Grace of God.

I am what I am.

I am justified, completely forgiven and made righteous.

I am dead.

I no longer live for myself.

I live for God.

I've been brought with a price.

I am not my own, but I belong to God.

I know I am established anointed and sealed in God by Christ.

I am His blessing.

I am given the Holy Spirit as a pledge, a guarantee as my inheritance.

I am crucified with Christ and it is no longer I who live but Christ.

Amen

Affirming The Grace of God To Me

I am chosen in Christ before the foundation of the world.

Predestined to be a son of God.

I am sanctified.

I am one with the sanctifier Christ.

He is not ashamed to call me brother.

I receive the spirit of God in my life,

that I might know the things given to me by God in Christ.

I have been redeem and forgiven.

I am a recipient of God's grace.

I decree He's been bruised for my iniquities.

The chastisement of His peace is upon me.

I have been given a spirit of power, of love, and self-discipline.

I've been saved and called according to God's doing.

I have a right to come bold to the throne

to find mercy and grace in the time of need.

Amen

Affirming The Promises of God

I confess I have been given exceedingly great and precious promises by God, which I am a partaker of his divine nature.

I have the mind of Christ.

I have obtained His inheritance.

I have overcome the World.

I have everlasting life and will not be condemned.

I have the peace of God which passes all understanding.

I have receive the power of the Holy Spirit.

The power to lay hand on the sick to see them recover.

The power to cast out Demon's.

The power over all power of the enemy.

I purpose to live so that I may approach God with boldness, freedom, and confidence.

I live by the law in spirit of Christ.

I walk in Christ Jesus.

I can do all things in Christ.

My life is hid in Christ and God I shall do greater works with the anointed one and His anointing Christ Jesus.

I shall over-come because greater is He who is in me, RIGHT NOW WORKING,

than He that is in this World.

So now I "PRESS" toward the mark of the prize of the high calling of God.

I will always Triumph.

The power of God is working in me.

In Jesus name.

Amen

We are commanded to pray for OUR Leader. Use this prayer to pray for you Pastors, Government officials, and those whom have rule over you!

Prayer For The Church and It's Vision

Father in the name of Jesus, we come into your presence, thanking you for Greater Harvest Christian Center and (<u>your churches name</u>). You have called us to be saints in our City and around the World.

As we lift our voices in one accord, we recognize that you are God and everything was made by you and for your Glory. We call into being, by our faith, those things that be not as though they were.

We thank you for our church family, our elders, ministers and leaders. We ask you to knot us together in our hearts, to be disciples to this ministry and for your Kingdom.

We agree to speak the same things as our Leaders teach us according to your word, because of our commitment to kindness and love towards each other. There is no division among us. We are perfectly joined together in the same mind. NO enemy can conquer or divide us,

We are united to stand for the Kingdom of God. Grant unto us, your Ambassadors here on this earth, a boldness to speak your word.

Favor us with new souls, signs and wonders, and a prosperous life because of our sharing of your gospel and your truths.

Therefore our minds, are alert to new souls needing comfort and to hear from you. We will direct them to this ministry work, which is the water and the word of life, which we seek after diligently.

We thank you for all our workmen, which are in abundance, and that we have all manner of gifted persons to help us with the labor and administration of this calling.

We also thank you because we share freely of our gifts and talents, and remove the yoke and weights from our Leaders, that we receive a special blessings.

Our labor of love does not go unnoticed by you Father, and you bless us at your hand because of this work. Each department operates in excellence.

Our Ministers are intercessors, standing in the gap for every member of this ministry. Therefore we are strong and mighty because of these prayers, and we pray for them also.

We have every gift we need to grow and become strong and be unified in the faith. None of our people will be like disobedient children, tossed to and fro, or carried about with every wind of doctrine.

We speak the truth and it is received with the love and correction of God. We want and desire the meat of the Word and ask our leaders, through prayer, to feed us with the truth of Gods word and we receive it in Grace and Love. Therefore we Grow and become a witnessing body of believers 100 strong.

We have every need met because our ministry seeks to be holistic, in spirit, mind, body, and soul.

Therefore we pledge to outreach pass our walls and expose our ministry to the community as an answer!

We ask for your wisdom Lord in meeting the needs of our community. We thank you Lord for open door opportunities to serve, and open door opportunities for our leaders to take your word to this nation.

Please grant our Apostle, Bishop, Pastor and our leaders open door opportunities to preach and teach your word to every nation. And we will support them in spirit and finances to spread your word to all.

We thank you for expanded ministry facilities that will more than meet our needs, and for enlarged territory as we continue to expand and grow.

We pledge our tithes and offerings in time, talent, and finances. Therefore our church is prospering financially and we have more than enough to meet our needs.

We have everything we need to reach this nation for Christ and to carry out your great commission by reaching this area and abroad for Jesus.

We are a people of Love as love is shed abroad in our hearts. We are a people of the Holy Spirit, Praise and Power. We are Kingdom Keepers.

We thank you for the Word of God living Big in all of us, and that Jesus is truly our Lord and Savior. We are an Extra Ordinary Church composed of Extra Ordinary People and doing Extra Ordinary Things.

We believe that we are operating in the realm of the Spiritual and will not operate as cardinal in the natural realm!

Thank you for your presence among us, the praise among us and your holiness among us.

We love you Lord and thank your for our Leaders. The Arch Bishop Rice, our Chief Apostle Dr. Rice, Pastor (<u>your pastors name</u>), our Leaders and our Staff. I am committed to this vision. It is where I know God has sent me to Grow.

Therefore I am like a tree planted by the rivers of living water, I am blessed to be a blessing to this ministry, and I will let nothing stop me from being that true blessing. Not myself or others. I am Committed, Steadfast, Unmovable, and always Abounding at the Greater Harvest Christian Center and (<u>your church name here</u>), therefore Praise and Joy are mine.

I lift my hand and Praise your Holy Name. I Shout Victory as I grow in the Kingdom of God.

I shout Victory as I take my Dominion.

(Shout VICTORY!!!)
 IN JESUS NAME

Amen

Chief Apostle Dr. J. G. Rice

My Declaration of Victory and Faith for Daily Living

In Christ I Am Anointed, I Am a Powerful-Person of GOD.I am the one that he has put his spirit in to overcome this world and all its pitfalls, are not in my path, for my steps are ordered my you and your word.

I decree I Am a Joint- Heir with Jesus and more than a conqueror. I have the sepulture of faith and I triumph in my daily walk with you father God, and I succeed through your son Christ Jesus today.

I put on the mind of you, Jesus today. I dress myself in your clothing and I anoint myself with your oil, my cup, my well, my table, my life, runneth over with the bounty of your provisions and your love.

You are my strength and you are my shield. I acknowledge you in all my ways and you direct my path.

I decree that I am a doer of the word of GOD, and a channel for His Blessing. I do not only purpose to hear the word but, to also apply it to my life as a living assignment.

I decree that I will continue to mature in Christ, and his word.

I decree I also mature in forgiveness and love.

I receive the spirit of Jehovah Mekodishkem, my sanctifier today.

I am created to be set apart for his Glory and his witness. Today I will live the life of evangelism and I will create a opportunity for someone to see Jesus in me today.

I decree I excel in wisdom, knowledge and understanding, they are my friends, my sisters and my trophies unto God.

I decree they have a place in my life of honor and respect.

I decree that the Spirit of living holy, Holiness, and Righteousness, Honor and Gods Glory also have respect today in my life.

I decree Goodness and the fruit of the spirit we honor you and respectively submit to you today.

In Jesus Name

Amen

Affirmations For My Spiritual Leaders

Father I recognize and thank you for my Spiritual Leaders and those who govern my life through your kingdom authority and sacrifices.

I speak to the winds of power, through Christ Jesus and ask you to send them a blessing of "Good Fruit" today as they continue to pour into my life. Bless them with all heavenly blessings and greatness.

I declare over my leader the spirit of ENDURANCE. May you push me, Father ROHI, and direct me to be a gift to them as you have made them a gift to me.

Teach me to hear their cry and to be a hand in the earth to help them to fulfill the vision that you have given them. Allow me to create smiles of happiness for my leader today, as they labor to fulfill your divine assignment on their lives.

I decree I am a blessing to my Leaders. I honor the 5 fold ministry persons in my life today. They are assigned to me through the InterGlobal body of believers of the nations. Bless the hands of their work as well.

I decree as a believer that you will bless them as you bless our church, ministry, and spiritual family as well.

I decree and pray for the Pastors, Missionaries, Ministry of Helps, Prophets, Psalmists, Praise Teams and Ministers of the Godly arts. All Deacons, Elders, Assistants to the kingdom keepers, and all Gods Ministers, a spirit of uncompromising leadership and an unlimited measure of Gods success, health, resources and covering over their lives.

I decree to all my brothers and sisters in Christ that you, as well as I, be blessed today, so much so that you as well shall, rise up and bless others.

I decree especially that my "Spiritual Leaders," my set Woman or Man of the Gospel, the ABUNDANCE OF SUCCESS on this day, right now. In the name of Jesus!

I declare them to receive the "Cyrus Anointing," the "Jabez Blessing" and the "Abraham Inheritance".

I declare that they are filled with multiplied blessings of grace, peace, mercy, favor, abundance, power, happiness, greatness, supernatural discounts, mighty moves of success, oneness with their loved ones, favor with kings and rulers of this land.

May our God grant Pastor _____ with strength for the assignment and overtaking joy, joy, joy. In the mighty name of Jesus our Lord

Move on my leaders behalf today in a great way. Keep them encouraged and full of patience, kindness, and temperance.

I declare Pastor _____ to be balanced enough to know when to ENGAGE in warfare, when to fight the war and to know when to live in peace. Father God, the giver of our gifts, every good and perfect leader is sent to us from you. I remind myself of this today!

I decree, I will never have an Absalom Spirit, as you are my helper. And if it is present in our ministry, Lord cast it out from among the flock of Christ Jesus Today.

I decree I have the wisdom to have a keen eye of discernment towards my spirit, and I will look for anything that is in me that will easily beset me and cause me to have my leader, our ministry, or the work of Christ as a whole to suffer.

God, our "NISSI", we pray to you today. Father God of Our

fathers, the God Of Israel, we ask you to never let us override our leader or abuse our Leaders for any reason or in any way. Rebellion has been in our mist since our Egyptian days,

I decree us to be free from the spirit that caused our fathers and mothers of old to fall and be swallowed up by the earth.

Jesus blood of Calvary!

RAPHA heal us and Remove rebellion from our hearts.

Do not let me become a vision or a leadership killer.

In Jesus Name

Amen

Decree For Growth In Christian Vision

ELOL- ELYON, help me grow the vision and walk with the vision of my leader.

I decree that you have called my leader and you gave them to me ADONAI, and I do submit to that plan from you for my life.

You are Jehovah Tsidkenu, the God of Righteousness. You never make a mistake. Therefore I will put my flesh and my mind under the subjection of your plan.

I decree that you, El Shammah, will cause them to lead me and your people with purpose and direction. Father grant Pastor _____ with an El Jireh Spirit. Allow it to flow down the beard to the body, as it is set to be upon our leader.

I decree you are Jehovah Shammah, and I declare that you will provide the funds to the vision. I am sent here to be a fund raiser and a Kingdom keeper.

I decree that through my help, the vision that you have given to our leader will not fail, die, or become dusty or delayed. Through the help of others and myself it shall flourish and stand tall and complete .

I recognize that what I pray for my leaders, I create a whirlwind of cycles to begin to happen for myself. So I pray for my leaders, the Spiritual feeders of my soul daily. That they will be filled completely with all spiritual necessities and the wealth of a great mind, a well of friends and with never ending joy.

As I have believed these things for my leader today, so I begin my day with a Promise of your word. Give and it shall be given unto me, good measure, pressed down and shaken over shall men give to my bosom.

I have given this prayer in faith, so others shall decree over my life goodness and greatness of your word today.

I receive it NOW!

In Jesus name.

Amen

Decree Of God's Love For Me

Father God, I decree over my life that you are for me, therefore nobody is bold enough to even think about coming against me. I am blessed coming in all my days and I am blessed going out all my days.

I have the "Midas Touch." Everything I touch is blessed.

I am ready now to gather in the harvest from the fields that I did not plant. To occupy the houses that I did not build. I receive the wealth of the wicked and I rejoice in the fact that you have prepared a place of rest for me.

I decree over my life that my enemies are fleeing before me. God has commanded his blessings on my store-houses. He has opened His good treasures and I shall lend and not borrow.

I decree over my life that God loves me. I am the head and not the tail.

I decree that God has given me the power to make wealth and I will operate in this powerful gift.

I dwell in the secret place of the information of God. He shares my future with me and guides me into a expected lace of safety. I have His protection and His provision.

God is My Refuge and my true fortress. I am not afraid of the snare of the fowler. No evil shall befall me and no plague shall come near me, my dwelling, or where ever I lay my head to rest, eat, sleep or enjoy life.

The Tormentor shall have no resting place with, in, or near me. The angel of the Lord assigned to me for my perfection shall trouble anyone or anything who tries to trouble me

God has given his angels charge over me and they are bearing me up and showing me my way in a clear path. Clearing out all obstacles today. My angels at this very moment are busy making sure my steps are blessed. I will not even dash my foot against a stone.

As declared according to the Holy word of God, which has rule over my life.

I live under the blood of Jesus and it prevails over my life today.

Amen

Decree of Establishment

1 Peter 2:9 established I am a chosen generation, a royal priesthood, a holy nation.

I am a peculiar person called out of darkness into His marvelous light.

I am God's favorite.

He cares for me today.

I smile because of his true love for me.

I have been healed by the stripes of Jesus from all cancer, diabetes, heart disease, any sickness, or afflictions, or infections, or any other diseases.

DESEASE you cannot and will not enter my body.

Today the Blood of Jesus protects me from any and all diseases, sickness and pains.

My Body, Mind, Spirit and Soul will respond to being "The Healed."

I am without spot or blemish, purified by the faith and confessions of my faith.

I am my own personal Intercessor.

I am the righteousness of God, saved and washed in the blood of Jesus.

I decree a thing of power and it happens for me.

My lips utter the praises of my Father Jehovah Jireh.

I am provided for today!

No weapon formed against me shall prosper.

Every tongue which rises up against me in judgment shall be condemned.

I destroy the forming of the weapon, it will destroy itself, in the forming, in the mist of the air.

It will crash and burn and return, to the sender void of its purpose to fulfill its destiny on their released words and their released and defeated warfare.

This is the heritage of the servants of the Lord.

In their righteousness, we shall triumph, we shall tread on every serpent, we shall be more than over comers, this promise is mine today.

It is for me "Say's" the Lord.

I am saved from wrath by Him and justified by the blood of the lamb.

Lord I pray to Love Jerusalem, and that peace be in her walls today.

I pray the blessings of Jerusalem over my life, my families lives, and my friends today. May those prosper that love Jerusalem, and that Peace will be within them and Prosperity in their houses.

This is my Confession.

This is what I believe.

I receive every word that has been spoken in the atmosphere.

I receive it NOW!!!

I walk in it NOW!!!

It shall come to pass, because I have spoken it. I
Believe it by faith in it is done.
In Jesus Name.
Amen

Affirmations of Great Success

I declare that I command this year to be my Best Year EVER, starting even again with today. The NOW anointing in my life shall ever increase my good path, which will cause me to collide with good people and they will grant me goodness out of their treasures of life. I speak a Ramah word into my life NOW, that will activate the goodness of this season in my life.

I take authority over this year. My season of planting last year, will bring forth a bumper crop of goodness towards me and in my favor this year. Good seeds that did not germinate last year will produce a great seed this year. My seed will not die, but will come forth to bless me in my life with great power. Today I reactivate my seeds of success.

I decree that all the elements of this year will corporate with me. I decree that these elemental forces shall refuse to corporate with my enemies. I speak to the moon, the sun, the stars, earth, water, and dry land. The balance of nature and spiritual things will cause and create the Glory of Favor to shine on me.

I am attractive to good things, good people, and great ideals. People who are not normally good to others, are very good to me, and pass others to bless me. The Greatness of the earth is my supplier and all the elements of great success are mine.

The creative forces of my mind and being are working together with the plan of the Father God and the heavenly host. I am surrounded by the Angels of God assigned to me to help me to my wealthy place.

The place of Joy in my life is abundant. Therefore all spheres are dominated with goodness, grace, excellence, wealth, riches, and prosperity for me and my life.

The life cycle elements are my friends. They must not smite me. I pull down every negative plan that is operating against my life this year. God has given my name a YES in high places.

This is the year that the lord has made, I will rejoice in it. The spirit of favor, counsel, might, power, wisdom, knowledge come upon me NOW! Rest with me this season, this day, and this cycle of great manifestation. Abide with me forever. May the Shalom of God, as I decree, fill my day like never before!

In Jesus name.

Amen

PRAYERS FROM THE ALTAR

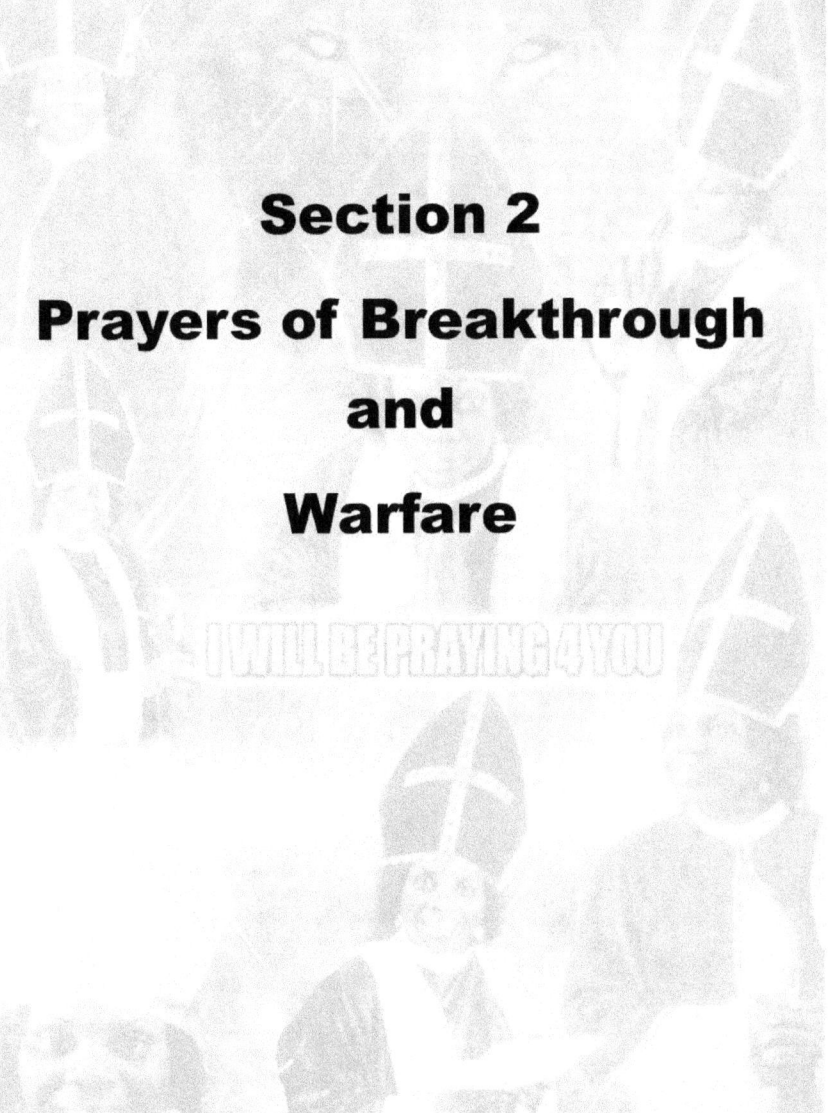

Section 2

Prayers of Breakthrough

and

Warfare

Section 2

Prayers of Breakthrough and Warfare

Breaking the Spirit of Deceptions	Page 93
Breakthrough Prayer: To Cast Out The Spirit of Deception	Page 95
Daily Prayer To Open The Gateways of Receiving Blessings	Page 96
Breakthrough Prayer For Power of Promotion and Expectation	Page 97
Breakthrough Prayer: The Heavens Will Arise in My Favor	Page 99
Breakthrough Prayer Over Difficult Things	Page 101
I Am A Mountain Of Praise: I Confess… These Scriptures	Page 102
Breakthrough Prayer For Promotion	Page 103
Breakthrough Prayer of Greatness For My Year	Page 104
Breakthrough Prayer to Attract Wealth	Page 105
Breakthrough Prayer to Destroy City/Area Blockades	Page 107
Breakthrough Prayer For My Entire Family	Page 108
Breakthrough Prayer for Great Health	Page 110
Breakthrough Prayer To Release…Impact Team	Page 112
Breakthrough Prayer to Unleash God's Power For Me	Page 113
Breakthrough Prayer to Overcome All Obstacles	Page 114
Breakthrough Prayer From Stubborn Pursuers	Page 116

NOTES

Breaking the Spirit of Deceptions

I set my heart, mind, body and soul to utter these Prayers from the Altar.

I DECREE and DELARE Jesus is Lord. Any breakthrough, will be easy and of no travail or difficulty! I break the Spirit and the Powers of Deception over my life TODAY, NOW and FOREVER MORE. In Jesus name.

I DECREE and DECLARE that all demonic opposition over me in these areas will cease now and forever more. I bind the enemy always from me. I will not be deceived or distracted any longer, in Jesus name! Let the teeth of the enemy over the affairs of my life break, in the name of Jesus. Let every evil covenant with the earth against my destiny be broken, in the name of Jesus.

Every input of curses in my destiny, die, in the name of Jesus. Every witchcraft padlock hanging against my destiny, break, in the name of Jesus. Let every evil covenant with the sun, moon and stars against my destiny to distract me be broken, in the name of Jesus. Let every evil covenant with the water against my destiny and future success be broken, in the name of Jesus.

Every witchcraft conspiracy over my destiny, through distraction and deception and their spiritual ties, be, scatter, in the name of Jesus. Thou power of stagnation and limitation, assigned against my destiny through Deception and Distractions, die, in the name of Jesus. Everyone who has accepted witchcraft for the sake of my destiny, and caused me to be tricked by deception and distractions be disgraced, in the name of Jesus.

Every evil power coming against my destiny through distractions and deception of people, family and others, die, in the name of

Jesus. You tree of failure in my family line, my destiny is not your candidate, die NOW! In the name of Jesus. Every pillar of witchcraft in my family line, that has opened the door to deception, lies and untruths be destroyed, in the name of Jesus.

O Lord, let the rivers of life and prosperity be released upon my dwelling place this year, this month, this week and this day, in the name of Jesus. I shall not be a spiritual casualty, deceiving myself through my own pattern of personal deception. Let my thoughts and my ways be guided by the Holy Spirit of Jesus Christ. Every Deception Spirit or Distraction Spirit will not be registered as bearing details of my destiny. Catch fire and lose track of me Now, by the blood of Jesus. Every evil image of Distraction or Deception, carved in my name, be roasted, in the name of Jesus.

O Lord, take away my portions from you, I will not be a casualty of destruction, deception and distraction for I will fulfill the divine purpose of my life, in growth, development and power, in the name of Jesus. My God, my life shall not be left with **the wind**s, but it will be glowing and growing forever in your grace and in your timing of favor for me.

I breakthrough new from all powers of Defeat and Distraction. The Spirit of Deception will not prevail in my life or in the lives of those assigned to be around me, to covenant with me, and to bless me! Witch, warlock, familiar spirits, or operations of evil, and ignorance used by this Beast of Despair, die NOW from my present, current or future trails and paths in the mighty name of Jesus.

I replace this spirit with wisdom, clear seeing revelation and prevailing truth. They now occupy and reign over all empty, cleared and abandoned space in my life. Set up righteous territories and fortresses in me.

In the name of Jesus. AMEN

Breakthrough Prayer: To Cast Out The Spirit of Deception

I pray now to outcast the Spirit of Deception, his friends and demonic foes from my life. I receive that my oath of prayer is now open, and I will operate as the "Soldiers' of Prayer" God has called us to be! We decree and declare God Jehovah, and his Son Christ Jesus, and the Holy Spirit as the head of our lives in these prayers. Therefore nothing shall by any means attack us or hurt us.

Deception, denial, delay and disloyalty, your assignment in our lives and any form of trickery be exposed to us NOW, in Jesus mighty name. Assignment to trick us, we expose you. Powers assigned to destroy our future, we confuse, cancel and reassign you, return to the sender to operate in their lives. We reveal every hidden motive and agendas before its season to come to fruit. Seed, die in the ground.

We now open our spirit for wisdom, understanding, and knowledge to bless our lives. We are his beloved and he abides in us. We are under the shadow of the Almighty; we have overcome by his blood. Any spirit that abides unlike the Father of Light will be exposed and dry up and die, in Jesus name, from our lives and our future.

We shall be free to be the matured children of the MOST HIGH GOD. We honor and respect the spirit of God that will only take us a high as we should go at any given time, and we will operate in truth and all peace, and the Love of the ALMIGHT GOD.

Our life is now in his hand and he will only expose to us what we can mentally, emotional, and physically handle. For our deliverance is at hand. We anoint ourselves with the oil of gladness and the garment of Praise is our weapon. To God be the Glory Great things he has done,

Now Father, in the name of Jesus, we expose deception and will not co-operate with his/her, nor cloak his/her garments, but we rend away from us, never to return anymore.

in Jesus name

Amen

Daily Prayer To Open The Gateways of Receiving Blessings

I believe and receive the blessing of God's GOODNESS today.

That it goes over my life, my family, our ministry, our Leaders, our family and friends.

Those who pray this prayer for me seen, and unseen, that now the "same blessings of God's goodness, is released by the Spirit of God, over us all, all who pray these prayers today!

Yes we decree, we are the "Prayer Ambassadors" for God, and we stand in agreement with each book holder, and Prayer Ambassador today and every day.

We are covered by the Blood of Jesus, and may Gods favor overtake us together, individually, and corporately for the kingdom of God.

Great doors are opened today for the believers of Faith.

That's Me! And I receive every good thing God has for us today.

I am not alone, someone is in agreement with me today in prayer, so I am Covered by the Blood of Jesus, the Only son of God.

I decree Goodness and Mercy follow us NOW, Peace goes before us, and Favor overtakes us NOW! in Jesus Name.

In Jesus name

Amen

Breakthrough Prayer For Power of Promotion and Expectation

Heavens lift up your sword and slay all spirit husbands/wives, in the name of Jesus. Any problem in my life caused by using my hair as a baby, die, in the name of Jesus.

Dark powers supervising my problems die, in the name of Jesus. Powers planted in my childhood to trouble my future, hear the word of the Lord, and die in the name of Jesus.

Marks on the body that appear and disappear, die in the name of Jesus. Every medicine, poured on the ground, to subdue my life, I destroy it now, in the name of Jesus.

I destroy the hand of every witchdoctor working against me, in the name of Jesus. Any blood sacrificed against me, let the life in the blood be revoked and smite them, in the name of Jesus.

Oh Life, that has been allowed to die through rituals against me arise now and strangulate your killers, in the name of Jesus. I quench every anger spirit released and energized through this land against me, in the name of Jesus.

By the power in the blood of Jesus, I subjugate the power of witches, in the name of Jesus. My prosperity shall not become history while I am still living, in the name of Jesus.

I break every unconscious agreement with the enemy, in the name of Jesus. I command, in Jesus Name, that Dark powers of corrupt and envious people over my life die, in the name of Jesus.

Back-up powers and replacement powers of the enemy dry up, in the name of Jesus. I cancel every astral assignment over my life, in the name of Jesus.

O God, arise and banish all the forces of evil from me, in the name of Jesus.

Polygamous curses troubling my life break now, in the name of Jesus. I cut off the horns of the wicked power by the power in the blood of Jesus.

Every serpent programming disgrace against me, I cut off your head in the name of Jesus. Every satanic altar in heaven and earth bearing my name, let them catch fire, in the name of Jesus.

Powers planting curses in my star die now, in the name of Jesus. I release my rising star from voodoo or fetish powers, in the name of Jesus.

O God, arise and release my blocked blessings, in the name of Jesus. I release the ten plagues of Egypt upon every coven troubling my life, in the name of Jesus. Woe unto every power assigned to stagnate me, in the name of Jesus.

Let the candle of the wicked be put out, in the name of Jesus. O God, distribute sorrow to all covens assigned against me, in the name of Jesus.

O God arise and let your anger be the breakfast, lunch and dinner to any power hired to curse me, in the name of Jesus. I release catastrophe and poverty upon any power assigned to rubbish my destiny, in the name of Jesus.

Ancestral debt collectors, release your hold, in the name of Jesus. Let desolation and destruction pursue my pursers, in the name of Jesus. Every voice that's releasing instructions to torment and hinder my life, die now, in the name of Jesus.

Warrior angels from heaven arise and lock up every satanic high priest troubling my life, in the name of Jesus. Negative powers, assigned to redesign my destiny, die, in the name of Jesus.

Every power mocking my God, die, in the name of Jesus. Every power challenging my destiny, die, in the name of Jesus.

The power of repeated problems, die, in the name of Jesus. Every power assigned to turn my glory to shame, die, in the name of Jesus.

Any poison in my body, die, in the name of Jesus. Blood of Jesus, open my gates of breakthroughs, in the name of Jesus.

Any sickness that wants to overtake my life, die, in the name of Jesus. My portion shall rule over my environment, in Jesus' name

I step into sudden wealth by fire, in the name of Jesus. Any power coming from behind to steal from me shall be buried alive,

in the name of Jesus.

AMEN

Breakthrough Prayer: The Heavens Will Arise in My Favor

O heavens, arise, connect me to my timing, in the name of Jesus. Burst forth my favor NOW, in Jesus name. O heavens, arise connect me to my destiny, in the name of Jesus. By fire, by thunder, by force, my blessings overtake me to victory, in the name of Jesus.

My mantle of dominion, fall upon me, in the name of Jesus. My Father, take away the trap of witchcraft from my head, in the name of Jesus. Strange words that are sent to trap me must scatter, in the name of Jesus. Hypnotic powers manipulating my life break away from me, in the name of Jesus. I declare an invasion of angels from heaven to scatter all covens, in the name of Jesus.

This month, hear the word of the Lord, swallow conspiracy, in the name of Jesus. Every evil pot raised up to control my life catch fire, in the name of Jesus. Worms from heaven consume every pot of witchcraft fashioned against me, in the name of Jesus. Every calendar fashioned against me, catch fire in the name of Jesus.

O God, release your wrath upon every power of witchcraft troubling my destiny, in the name of Jesus. O God, arise and root them out of their land in your anger, in the name of Jesus. O God, arise and cast your fury upon agents of affliction troubling my star, in Jesus' name.

Candle of the wicked, I put you out. Quench all information stored in the caldron against me, in the name of Jesus. I release panic and havoc upon any gathering summoned to disgrace me. I release confusion and backwardness upon every satanic programmer attacking my star, in the name of Jesus.

Every cage formed to imprison my star; I smash you, in the name of Jesus. I release the ten plagues of Egypt upon every coven tormenting my existence. Thou that exalted yourself as an eagle against me, I knock you down. Every ancestral debt collection, be silenced, in the name of Jesus. Every locker and warehouse holding my blessings of wealth, catch fire, in Jesus' name

Invisible wall of barriers stagnating my destiny, scatter now. Invisible barricades stagnating my goals, scatter now. Every trap that repeats evil circles, catch your owner, in the name of Jesus.

Snare of right place at the wrong time, break by fire, in the name of Jesus. Snare of being one day late, one dollar short, break, in the name of Jesus. Spring BREAK in Jesus name. Snare of too little, too late, break, in the name of Jesus. Loose your trap in Jesus name.

Prayers of Jabez to provoke my enlargement, manifest in my life, in the name of Jesus.

Prayers of Cyrus, benefit me NOW, in the name of Jesus.

I WILL succeed TODAY and have BREAKTHROUGH by the forces of Heaven.

In Jesus name

AMEN

Breakthrough Prayer Over Difficult Things

O Lord, DO a GLORIOUS thing in my life before the close of this year, this month, this week, this day, and this season. That will make every ear that hears of your goodness towards me tingle,

IN THE NAME OF JESUS.

O God that doeth hard things, Dissolve every difficult problems of my life by fire. By the key of effectual and fervent prayer, I open the heavens over my destiny after the order of Elijah. Therefore, O rain of my glory, Begin to fall upon my destiny now before the end of this month,

IN THE NAME OF JESUS.

You the cloud of the desert that carries no water for my destiny, your time is up. Scatter unto desolation. My angelic helpers, wherever you are, I loose you and unleash you to execute the divine assignment of God for my life this year, Clouds of Gain and Goodness burst forth NOW over my life, beginning with this week

IN THE NAME OF JESUS

O key of David, open the heavens over my family, career, ministry and the labor of my hands. Every king Uzziah blocking the heavens over my life, Your time is up!

DIE! DIE!! DIE!!!

IN THE NAME OF JESUS.

God has me on His mind for blessings. I shall manifest His glory in this earth. Difficulties be dismantled, dethroned, and dejected, NOW, by the blood and in the name of Jesus Christ of Nazareth. Be replaced by perfect timing, connection, and divine spot lights on my life to cause others who wish to find me, to bless me, to see the light. Others of no good, to my success and wealth, be blinded, NOW, by the light of Glory.

IN JESUS NAME

AMEN

I Am A Mountain Of Praise

I Confess and Decree These Scriptures

Isaiah 25:6

"That in this mountain shall the LORD of hosts make unto all people a feast of fat things, a feast of wines on the lees, of fat things full of marrow, of wines on the lees well refined."

Isaiah 25:7

"Jehovah God will destroy in this mountain the face of the covering cast over all people, and the veil that is spread over all nations."

Isaiah 25:8-9

"The Great I Am will swallow up death in victory; and the Lord GOD will wipe away tears from off all faces; and the rebuke of his people shall he take away from off all the earth: for the LORD hath spoken it... And it shall be said in that day, Lo, this is our God; we have waited for him, and he will save us: this is the LORD; we have waited for him, we will be glad and rejoice in his salvation."

Luke 12:6-7

"I decree that five sparrows sold for two pennies? And not one of them is forgotten before God. Why, even the hairs of your head are all numbered. Fear not; you are of more value than many sparrows."

Isaiah 25:3

"I decree the strong people glorify thee, the city of the terrible nations shall fear thee."

Isaiah 25:10

"I decree this mountain shall the hand of the LORD rest, and Moab shall be trodden down under him, even as straw is trodden down for the dunghill."

Breakthrough Prayer For Promotion

My ladder of promotion and glory, what are you doing in the hands of my enemies?

Arise! Break-Free!! And locate me now by fire!

In the name of Jesus!

Every ladder of infirmity sponsored by the devil against my prosperous health this year, catch fire and burn to ashes!

In the name of Jesus!

By the ladder that carried Joseph from the prison of Portiphar to the Palace of Pharaoh. O God Arise, and catapult me from persecution to my throne this year.

In the name of Jesus!

You, the key of my promotion, which the enemy has thrown into the river and in custody of marine witchcraft. Hear the verdict of Fire! I withdraw you from the cage of the strong man, and by you I flung open the gates of my glory to shine forth!

In Jesus name!

Where is the Lord God of Elijah? Arise and promote me by fire,

NOW!!!

I receive my breakthrough to be promoted. The wicked shall not prosper in my sight, and I fail not.

Promotions come NOW!!!

In the name of Jesus.

Amen

Breakthrough Prayer of Greatness For My Year

O Lord, my God, by your power that opened rivers in high places, I decree and declare the power of God to open the Gates of Heaven this year. Let the Gate of Blessing this year (current year) be OPEN BY FIRE to my prosperity, favor, good health, abundance and benefit this entire year, and let it flood my wilderness! In Jesus name!

I prophesy to the gates of poverty and shame operating in my life. I am not your captive in (current year), therefore, VANISH BY FIRE! In Jesus name! You the prison doors of infirmity (identify and mention that ailment by its name) blocking my health and wellness in (current year), CRUMBLE to dust under my feet! In the name of Jesus.

Ancient gates of powerlessness, of my father's house, assigned to afflict me in (current year), be wasted by the power in the blood of Jesus! Inherited weaknesses of my father's house, I issue a quit notice to you this year. Vacate my life now! In the name of Jesus.

Every gate my ancestors have opened in my foundation to capture my honor and glory. I render you impotent and shut you up by the power in the blood of Jesus. Rivers in high places, flow down and turn my dry valley into a fountain of pool of water this year. In the name of Jesus. I unleash the power of God to go forth before me this year and loose the loins of kings for my sake! In the name of Jesus.

My Father, hold my right hand throughout this year to subdue nations. Make me a global champion.

In Jesus name!

Amen

Breakthrough Prayer to Attract Wealth

Wealth of nations! From the North, South, East and West. Arise with urgency and locate my destiny this year! In the name of Jesus. Every gate of brass erected to stop my breakthroughs this year, I command you to break to PIECES! Floodgate of divine power, overshadow me this year. In the name of Jesus.

Bars of iron on mission to hinder my testimonies this year, scatter asunder and receive disgrace! I unleash the divine contingency of God to arrest every satanic emergency programmed against me and my family this year. Amen! In the name of Jesus.

Speak woe to every strongman of the strong city that is resisting my entry to my promised land this year! Move over, accept me, attract the greatness of your city, area, space and place to favor me, in the name of Jesus.

From this hilltop altar, I speak death to every victory which the enemy has had over my life in the past! Power shall change hands, NOW, to me and those who fight for me, forever and this day. In the name of Jesus.

O God of vengeance, let your hands of fire rest for me. That you may tread down the wicked strongman of my father's house, like straw is trodden down in the dunghill. This year, I shall drink the wines of victory from the cup of Jehovah, the Man of War, to celebrate my conquest of the strong city! In the name of Jesus.

Every veil covering my angels eyes to prevent them from conquering the strong city, be destroyed on this mountain of God and catch fire! O Lord of Hosts, let your fear and your dread fall upon my adversarial strongman. Let him turn his back and flee.

In Jesus name.

This year, the Lord shall wipe away my age-long tears from my face. O God arise and wipe tears of failure and sorrow from my face. Replace them with tears of joy unspeakable, full of glory! I speak from my covenant position on the hilltop of Zion, Moriah, Tabor, Hebron, Garmel and mount Nebo.

In Jesus name.

I command every valley of shame and sorrow to be filled with joy unspeakable, full of glory. Every city cooking my destiny in a cauldron of failure, I command that cauldron to break to pieces. Let my life spring up speedily from the valley of frustrations unto the mountain of success and breakthroughs! In the name of Jesus.

Every power of the valley pulling me from the mountain of glory, loose your grip on me and die by fire! I prophesy unto the four winds to go with holy fire and enter into the very dry bones of my destiny. Today I breakthrough to attract wealth to my life. I revive and resurrect into an exceeding mighty army to conquer my strong city and take their spoils to my lot and land. City keeper yield now to the voice of God to bless me, provide substance, land, houses and wealth to me freely for Kingdom Inhabitance. I exchange poverty for wealth, NOW!

In Jesus name.

Amen

Breakthrough Prayer to Destroy City/Area Blockades

You, Jehovah Sabaoth, are the exceeding mighty army of my destiny,

ARISE and overthrow every oppression and oppressor

that is hindering my success and breakthrough this year!

In the name of Jesus.

You are the RULING CITY!

The God of Zion, you are the one that is SET UP on a HILL.

The strong city should obey you and answer to you.

You are the Commanding City of God.

No city, strong or weak, should capture you.

I am the light of God in a dark world.

I am the center of His plan for the world.

This world is made for praise, we are not made for the world.

Through my prayers, I now command the minor city to know its place under the City of Praise.

Today, I lay hold of the key of David by fire!

Let the doors of greatness, prosperity and health, open unto me by fire.

Let every door of failure, tragedy and infirmities, shut down by fire!!!

In the name of Jesus.

Amen

Breakthrough Prayer For My Entire Family

I decree intercession and standing in the gap for my family, NOW, in the name of Jesus. By the blood of Jesus, I deliver my family tree from serpent and scorpion, in the name of Jesus. Every satanic termite, operating inside my family tree, dry up and die, in the name of Jesus. By the blood of Jesus and Holy Ghost fire, purge the foundation of every member of my family, in the name of Jesus. I lift up the (family name) family and all its generations to come. Architect and builders of affliction, in the family line, scatter, in the name of Jesus.

Every power of negative like father like son, like mother like daughter, clear away by the power in the blood of Jesus. In the name of Jesus, I ruin the power of every strongman assigned to trouble my blood line. Every agent of wickedness in my bloodline, I bind and cast you out with all your roots, in the name of Jesus. Every curse, evil covenants and enchantments militating against the star of my family, die, in the name of Jesus. Strongmen behind stubborn problems in my family line, die, in the name of Jesus.

Anything buried or planted in my family compound, that is reactivating ancient demons, catch fire, in the name of Jesus. Any evil tree planted anywhere, that speaks against my destiny, dry to the roots, in the name of Jesus. Satanic panel, set up against my family line, scatter, in the name of Jesus. Any evil harvest invading my family line, be cancelled by the blood of Jesus. Every power base of darkness, supervising any problem in my family line, dry up, in the name of Jesus.

O Lord, change my present speed and grant me new speed, in the name of Jesus. Oh God arise with you divine medication and heal my family tree, in the name of Jesus. Oh God arise with your sword of fire and deliver my family tree, in the name of Jesus.

Every trend of infirmity, sickness and iniquity, flowing through my family lineage, be arrested by the power in the blood of Jesus.

Any consequence of any evil covenant that my forefathers have entered into, break now, in the name of Jesus. All vows against me from the roots, die, in the name of Jesus. The benefits of my father's house, stored in marine, forests or rocky warehouses, be released, in the name of Jesus. I decree the battles that defeated my parents, shall not defeat me, in the name of Jesus.

Archives of darkness, release my beneficial information, in the name of Jesus. Sodomites, Philistines, Ammonites, Hittites or Jezebites Spirits, die, NOW. Every satanic handwriting and ordinances, speaking against my family line, die by fire, in the name of Jesus. Ancestral secrets behind my problem, be revealed, in the name of Jesus. Every dark power afflicting my family line, scatter, in the name of Jesus

All vows against me from the roots, die, in the name of Jesus. The benefits of my father's house, stored in marine, forests or rocky warehouses, be released, in the name of Jesus. I command the belly of any ancient serpent that has swallowed the virtues of my family to burst and release them, in Jesus' name. Any evil pronouncement and decrees, fastened to the heavenlies against my family line, be wiped off by the blood of Jesus. Wipe your face and say, I refuse to sweat in vain, in the name of Jesus.

The battles that defeated my parents, shall not defeat me, in the name of Jesus. Thou Great Physician, Jehovah Rapha, heal every injury and wounds on my family tree, in the name of Jesus. Every information stored in the caldron against my family, catch fire, in the name of Jesus. All information stored in the memory bank of the enemy against my family tree, be wiped off by the blood of Jesus. Angels of fire, locate my family roots and uproot all arrows of wickedness, in the name of Jesus.

Holy Ghost fire, purge my roots for breakthrough repositioning, in the name of Jesus. Inherited weaknesses, clear away by the blood of Jesus, in the name of Jesus. Jesus allow any family member trapped in darkness, dark places, or dark things, the Angel of Light frees you, NOW! Never to return again. Failure, drugs, sex, money, ungodly lifestyles, we oppose you, NOW. Uproot yourselves from among us. In the name of Jesus.

Yokes hanging on my family tree, break, in the name of Jesus. Coven cages tracking down the stars of my family, break and backfire. Boomerang! Stop, uproot, convert to ashes, die now, in the name of Jesus. In its place I call forth Salvation, Honor, Glory, Peace, Unity, Love, Kingdom Citizens, Grace, Mercy and Favor of NOW, Overtaking Blessings, Joy and God's Forgiveness and Power on my entire family! We shall prevail socially, spiritually and economically, in Jesus name.

The (<u>family name</u>) family shall live in abundance and declare the works of the Lord generationally and forever. The sealed covenant shall not return void, in the mighty name of Jesus. Long life , great strength, wealth, good health, beauty and grace, abiding in the House of the Lord, shall be our portion of the Lord from this day forth.

Each year we shall increase in our portion. Each day we shall flourish in our inheritance. Power, strength, might, social influence, gatekeeper favor, prayer and prophetic strength shall abide over the (<u>family name</u>) family today and forevermore. Abundance, great joy, peace love, singing, preaching, and Apostolic authority belongs to the (family name) family. In the mighty name of the Great I Am, Jehovah God, Yeshewa Lord, and the Angels will manifest our blessing daily and forevermore. In the name of Jesus

Amen

Breakthrough Prayer for Great Health

I decree and declare this prayer for prevailing health in my life today. Thou Great Physician, heal every disease on my family tree, in the name of Jesus. Blood of Jesus, wash and purge my family tree, in the name of Jesus. Swallowers and emptiers, loose your hold upon our family tree, in the name of Jesus. Opportunity wasters, targeting my family tree, be shaking off by the power in the blood of Jesus.

Curses troubling my family tree, be broken, in the name of Jesus. Lord Jesus, walk back to my day and place of birth, in the name of Jesus. Any power trading with the virtues of my family tree, release them now, in the name of Jesus. Star hunters and observers of times, targeting my family star, receive blindness, in the name of Jesus. Backwardness and failure of my father's house and of my mother's house, be eliminated, in the name of Jesus.

The horns assigned to torment my lineage and demote them, die, in the name of Jesus. Every root bearing gall and wormwood in my family tree, be washed by the blood of Jesus, in the name of Jesus. Thou pursuing arrows, tormenting my family, backfire, in the name of Jesus. Power of Leviathan and the sea, release my family, in the name of Jesus. Virtues buried with any dead relative that is affecting my progress, resurface by fire, in the name of Jesus. My Father, use me to change my family history, in the name of Jesus.

God of Elijah, send down your purging fire and sanitize my family tree, in the name of Jesus. Every satanic handwriting against my family, dry up, in the name of Jesus. Every gathering of ancient demons against my family tree, scatter, in the name of Jesus.

O Lord, as you did with Jannes and Jambres, in the days of Moses, confound the omens of enchanters and sorcerers challenging my shining, in the name of Jesus. O God arise, render diviners mad, make fool of them and make their dark knowledge foolishness, in the name of Jesus. Make those speaking against my health be put to an open shame. May they be afflicted by their shame.

I rebuke and dismantle satanic alliances and confederations battling my destiny, in the name of Jesus. Let every clandestine effort and endeavor fashioned against me and my health scatter unto desolation, in the name of Jesus. I disappoint the devices of the crafty so that their hands cannot perform their enterprise, in the name of Jesus.

O God, arise and take the enemies in their own crafty and devious ways. My Father, send divine angelic warriors to scatter the every diabolical intelligence programmed to stop me, by sending my body affliction. Every satanic database compiled against me, be consumed and destroyed, in the name of Jesus.

My Father, arise in your mercy and blot out all diabolical records organized against me. Archives of darkness, release my beneficial information, in the name of Jesus. Every satanic handwriting and ordinances, speaking against my health, die by fire. Ancestral secrets behind my problem are revealed, my health shall flourish, in the name of Jesus. My DNA will renew itself, my strength will rebound. Every dark power afflicting my family line, scatter, in the name of Jesus. I release myself from all problems originating from the mistakes of my ancestors, in the name of Jesus.

I decree my health shall spring forth like the morning sun. Mercy is now for me this morning. My DNA shall not hold any negative data, but shall return to youthful renewal daily. My liver and my colon shall renew, repair and replace itself with great strength. My eyes, skin, hearing and heart shall operate with youthful replacement and function. Today I am healed by the stripes of Jesus. My feet, legs, back and arms are proven for strength daily. My mind is in perfect peace. My soul rests in Jesus Christ. I am Gods golden vessel, I will not grow old, cold or tarnish. I shall serve the Kingdom of God in perfect strength. Amen.

Breakthrough Prayer To Release and Invoke My Heavenly Impact Team

Lord, let my words matter in heaven, in Jesus name. O Lord, promote me to fight in the heavenlies. All the champions of evil, I stone your foreheads, in the name of Jesus. O Lord, let the stars fight against every witchcraft bird assigned against me. Let the sword of the Lord, arise and dislodge every evil program in the heavens. Any power opposing the purpose of God for my life, be shifted away, in the name of Jesus.

All satanic investments, be shaken out of the heavenlies, in the name of Jesus. Let every power opposing the prophetic agenda for my life be dismantled. I prophesy over my life, (mention your name), wake up. Every agenda of bewitchment, be shaken off. I pull down every dominion in the heavenlies working against me. Let the sun and moon expel all evil plantations against me. Let the stars fight against my enemies, in the name of Jesus. O Lord, subdue kings, peoples, sorceries, enchantments, for my sake, in the name of Jesus.

Every horn of darkness, planning to scatter my life, scatter, in the name of Jesus. O Lord, maximize your altar in my life. I scatter every evil confrontation. Anything in my life, that is making the enemy to ask where is my God, receive divine solution. O Lord, set a remembrance for me and my family, in the name of Jesus. Every altar, mounted against my destiny, in the heavenlies, be dismantled. The shadow of my background will not cut me off, in the name of Jesus.

O Lord, re-open my life unto breakthroughs. Let my Heavenly Impact Team fight for me. O Lord, let every accusation in the heavenlies against me be broken. O Lord, purge sickness out of my life. The devil will not bury me, in the name of Jesus. I paralyze every activity of wickedness in the heavenlies against me. I decree, by covenant with the father El Shaddia, that every satanic information, registered in the heavenlies against me, be nullified now, today and forever. I command all the days left in this year to favor my life, in the name of Jesus. The sun will not smite me by day, nor the moon by night, rather, they will arise and fight for me, in the name of Jesus.

I receive power to mount up with wings as Eagle, NOW, in the name of Jesus. O heavens, arise in the thunder of your power and pursue my pursuers, in the name of Jesus. Any power, drawing power from the heavenlies against me, be crushed, in the name of Jesus. My Father, arise for my sake and let me advertise your power. Every power of Sisera, pursuing my destiny, I strike your forehead with the nail of fire, in the name of Jesus. Father, let Your angels arise and convene my breakthroughs to me, in the name of Jesus. Holy Ghost fire, sanitize every part of my life and environment. Let my Heavenly Impact Team move on time and under El Shaddai's agenda for me, NOW, in the name of Jesus.

Amen

Breakthrough Prayer to Unleash God's Power For Me

I decree I am unleashing Gods power to go forth on my behalf.
I unleash the power of God to go forth before me this year.

EVERY DAY,

EVERY WEEK,

EVERY MONTH,

EVERY SECOND,

AND EVERY HOUR OF EVERY DAY.

Blessings be stirred in the wind for me and in my favor.
Arise and Arrive QUICKLY and come to my hast.

Favor with people who have influence over my destiny, times, or seasons.

Peace rest on each person head that will hear my name.
A sweet smelling savor will arise concerning me and a right now urge to bless me.

Forgive me of any debt or cause against me.
Anything concerning me will be judged in my favor from this day forth, by the blood of Jesus Christ!

The conquering one whom has made me to be more than a conqueror through his name.

Therefore I decree favor on me, and loose the loins of kings towards me in goodness, kindness, strength and mercy for my sake!

In the name of Jesus!

My supervisors and those in authority over me will, must, and shall grant me exceptional favor, in the name of Jesus.
Today, Gods power goes forth for me!

Amen

Breakthrough Prayer to Overcome All Obstacles

I decree I am an over comer. God has created me to do something destined for Him. He has committed into my hand some assignments which He has not committed to anybody else. He has NOT created me for nothing.

I shall do GOOD. I shall do His WORK. I shall be an agent of PEACE and BLESSING. I will TRUST Him in whatever I do and whatever I am. I can NEVER be thrown away or down-graded. There will be no POVERTY of body, soul, spiritual, or finances in my life.

This year the anointing of God upon my life give me FAVOR in the eyes of God and men, all the days of my life. I shall NOT labor in vain. I shall walk this year in VICTORY, ABUNDANCE, and LIBERTY of spirit.

This year the Lord will make me a WINNER, a candidate of uncommon testimonies. This year I receive daily prayer, GOOD SEEDS to sow every-time, and money to spend ALWAYS. In this year my life will display the GLORY of God, in the name of Jesus.

I cancel all appointments with SORROW. I cancel all appointments with TRAGEDY. I cancel all appointments with EVIL CRIES, in the name of Jesus. This year I will encounter and experience a full scale of LAUGHTER, in the name of Jesus.

As for now on, blood thirsty demons and robbers will FLEE from my presence. Where ever I am, in the seat, in the air, on the road, the evil forces will BOW to my authority. Anything I have waited for till now, for a longtime, shall come and shall

MARVELOUSLY appear, in the name of Jesus. My expectation for Gods goodness to me is great today.

My father makes me and my family completely IMMUNE to any sickness or diseases this year, in the name of Jesus. This year I put myself, my family, my church members and all Greater Harvest Christian Center (your churches name) partners, in the PROTECTIVE envelope of divine favor, in the name of Jesus.

This year I will do the WILL of God and I will SERVE God, in the name of Jesus. This year I will have incomparable VICTORY, in the name of Jesus. This year, like clay in the hands of the potter, the Lord will make what He wants out of my LIFE, in the name of Jesus.

This year the Lord will do with me WHATEVER He wants, in the name of Jesus. This year the Lord will make me the HEAD and not the TAIL, in the name of Jesus. This year every snare of the fowler that is assign against me shall perish, NOW.

This year I render the HABITATION of darkness assigned against me VOID. This year divine DEPOSIT shall settle in my life, in the name of Jesus.

This year I enter the COVENANT of favor, in the name of Jesus. This year the anointing of SUCCESS and FRUITFULLNESS shall rest on me. This year I will not be a candidate of sweating with no RESULTS.

This year all obstacles on my way of progress shall be DISMANTLED. By the Power and Blood of God, I decree this breakthrough in my life. I receive it, NOW. In the awesome name of Jesus.

Amen

Breakthrough Prayer From Stubborn Pursuers

This year my God shall rise and my stubborn pursuers shall scatter, in the name of Jesus. This year those that mocked me in the pass shall celebrate me NOW, in the name of Jesus. This year my Goliath shall experience destruction, in the name of Jesus. This year every power assigned to cut short my life shall die NOW, in the name of Jesus. This year my prayer shall provoke excellent power. This year I shall speak and my words shall bring testimonies.

Oh thou that trouble me, they will have to fight against the God of Elijah, and he shall trouble them TODAY. Every one of my enemies shall scatter NOW, in Jesus name. Oh God arise and up-root everything you did not plant inside Greater Harvest Christian Center (your Church's name), Apostle and Bishop Rice (your Pastor's name) and our members and partners, in the name of Jesus.

Let the fire of revival fall NOW upon Greater Harvest Christian Center (your Church's name), Apostle and Bishop Rice (your Pastor's name), our members, and our partners. Let it fall NOW!!!

Let us become the blessed and the blessing. Let us become the head and not the tail.

And let us experience the power of our Lord and Savior Jesus Christ.

THE YOKE DESTROYING! THE BURDEN REMOVING! THE BLESSING RESTORING! THE MIRACLE WORKING POWER OF GOD!

Let it happen NOW!

My body, my soul, my mind, my spirit is in agreement.

In Jesus name. Amen.

NOTES

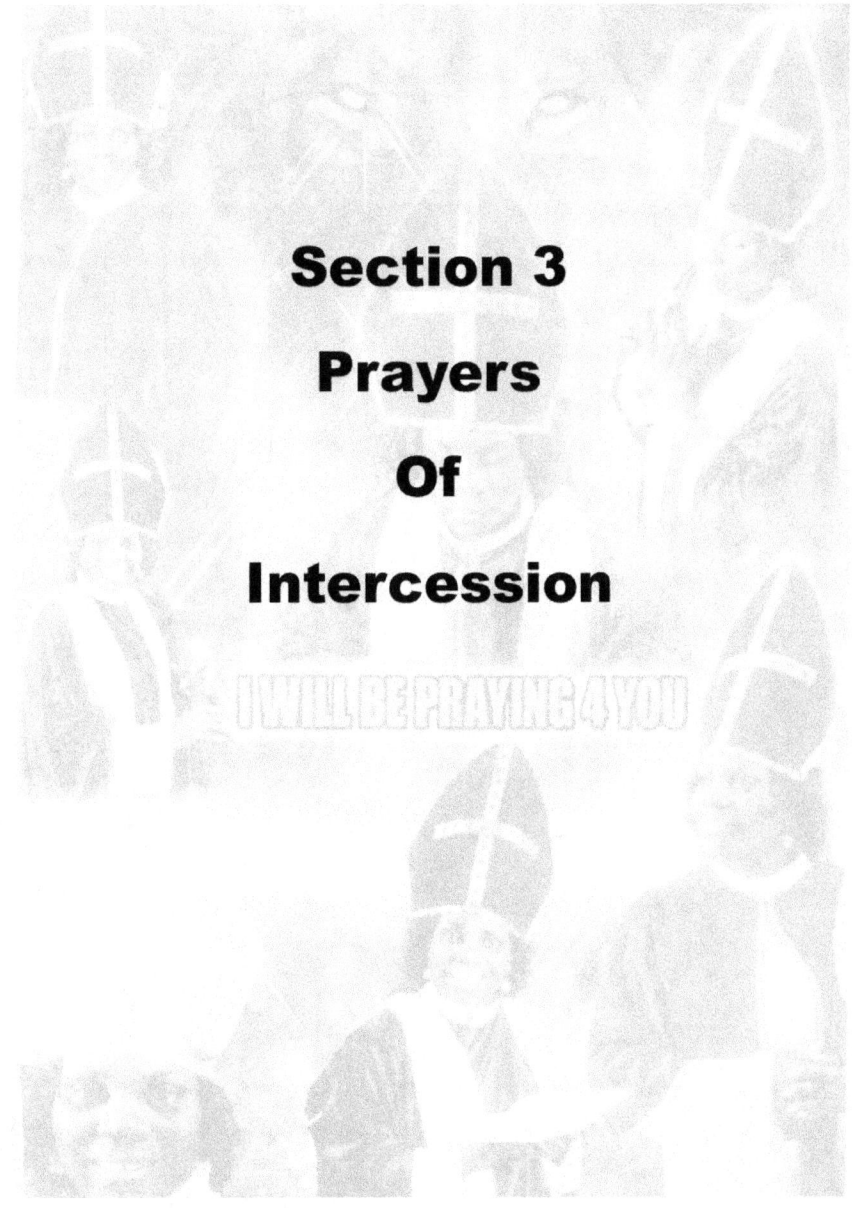

Section 3
Prayers
Of
Intercession

Section 3

Prayers

Of

Intercession

Prayer to Business, Great Personal Motivational Success and Family Greatness	Page 135
The Prayer of Psalm 91	Page 137
The Healing Decree	Page 140
Prayer to Invoke My Angelic Benefits: Blessings	Page 142
Prayer to Invoke My Angelic Benefits: Deliverance	Page 144
Prayer to Invoke My Angelic Benefits: Promotion	Page 146
Prayer to Invoke My Angelic Benefits: Protection	Page 148
Prayers to Invoke My Angelic Benefits: Waging War Against the Enemy	Page 150
Prayers to Invoke My Angelic Benefits: Dislodge Evil	Page 152
Prayers to Invoke My Angelic Benefits: Dismantle Evil Agendas	Page 153
Prayers to Invoke My Angelic Benefits: Dismantling by Fire	Page 155
I Release the Spirit of Rest and Peace on my Journey	Page 157
The Resurrection Power Prayer	Page 161
The Prayer of Public Success	Page 164
Confessions For My Bloodline As An Intercessor	Page 166
Prayer of Spiritual Renewal and Restoration	Page 169

NOTES

Prayer to Business, Great Personal Motivational Success and Family Greatness

I decree I will excel this year in business, in spiritual growth, in retention of God's word, and in great motivational thoughts that will fill me with a good mental awareness of sound practices.

I will read at least 3 motivational books per year that will help me to go to my full wealthy place. I decree my Loyalty to Jesus Christ and his mission here on earth. There is nothing that shall defile me. I decree I am possessing the gates of my enemies.

The Lord Jesus Christ shall anoint me with the oil of gladness. I will not be sad or dismayed by the reason of the great multitudes. The battle is never mines. I decree it is already fought, won and over. Therefore I rest in the peace of knowing that the Greater One, the Only True and Living God (YAHWEH), the Great I am, through his Son Christ Jesus, has already won the battle and given me the spoils. The gold and silver, and coal and oil, diamonds, and rubies are mine. All mine. Upon my fellows mankind, I release the same word of Peace and blessings.

I prepare myself to occupy my wealthy place. One day will make a change in my status. My breakthrough to my wealthy place will come NOW! With the suddenly anointing, the Cyrus expectation shall overtake me! I decree in just one quick meeting in time, the power of riches shall be bestowed on me for the blessing of the kingdom through my hand. The fire of the enemy shall not burn me, or disappoint me .

I decree I will condition my ears to hear greatness. No scams or unproductive chatter will I hear. My ears shall hear good news. My mouth shall not detour me through being ignorant or unlearned. I will not sabotage my own blessings. I decree I shall speak with the wisdom of God, and the favor of man shall befall me. I shall not hear the voice of the enemies nor their plans. What they may or may not say and think is not relevant. My future is secure in Christ. In his words of faith do I completely trust.

I decree today that my mind is fixed, my heart made up, that I will not die broke or broken. I shall live long, be healthy, and fulfill the plan and purpose for my life. In Jesus name, I will leave a legacy that others will know and remember the God of my salvation.

In the mighty name of Jesus, I decree you are good and your mercy endures forever in Jesus Name. I start my day with power. I bless my day with Grace. I cover my day with the Blood of Jesus. I fill my day with the Love of Jesus. I am prepared for a good day. In Jesus name

Amen

The Prayer of Psalm 91

I take authority over this year, in the name of Jesus. I decree that all the elements of this year will cooperate with me. I decree that these elemental forces should refuse to cooperate with my enemies.

I speak unto the sun, the moon and the stars. They must not smite me. I pull down every negative energy planning to operate against my life this year. This is the year the Lord has made, I will rejoice and be glad in it.

I dismantle any power uttering incantations to capture this year. I render such incantations and satanic prayers null and void. I retrieve this year out of their hands, in the name of Jesus. Spirits of favor, counsel, might and power, come upon me, in the name of Jesus.

I shall excel this year and nothing shall defile me. I shall possess the gates of my enemies. The Lord shall anoint me with the oil of gladness above my fellows. The fire of the enemy shall not burn me. My ears shall hear good news and I shall not hear the voice of the enemy.

My future is secured in Christ, in the name of Jesus. God has created me to do some definite services. He has committed into my hands some assignments which He has not committed to anybody. He has not created me for nothing.

I shall do good. I shall do His work. I shall be an agent of peace. I will trust Him in whatever I do and wherever I am. I can never be thrown away or downgraded. There will be no poverty of body, soul and spirit in my life this year.

The anointing of God upon my life gives me favor, in the eyes of God and man, all the days of my life. I shall not labor in vain. I shall walk this year in victory and liberty of the spirit.

This year, the Lord will make me a winner and a candidate of uncommon testimonies, in the name of Jesus. This year, I receive daily bread, good seed to sow every time, and money to spend always, in the name of Jesus.

In this year, my life will advertise the glory of God, in Jesus' name. I cancel all appointments with sorrow, tragedy and evil cry this year, in the name of Jesus. This year, I will encounter and experience a full scale laughter in all fronts, in the name of Jesus.

As from now on, blood-thirsty demons and robbers will flee at my presence, in the name of Jesus. Whether I am on the sea, in the air or on the road, the evil forces there will bow to my authority, in the name of Jesus.

Anything I have waited for till now, for a long time, shall be miraculously delivered to me this year, in the name of Jesus. My Father, make me and my family members completely immune to any form of sickness or disease this year, in the name of Jesus.

This year, I put myself and members of my family into the protective envelope of divine fire, in the name of Jesus. This year, I will do the will of God and I will serve God, in the name of Jesus. This year, I will have unconquerable victory.

Any power pressing my head down, I shake you into the fire of God, in the name of Jesus. I speak to my mind to TRANSFORM into the newness of CHRIST Satanic agents, assigned to stop me, I stop you before you stop me, in the name of Jesus. Satanic coma or full stop, assigned to detain me, vanish, in the name of Jesus. Opportunity aborters, I puncture your powers, in the name of Jesus. Every altar of satanic delay, catch fire, in the name of Jesus.

My hidden treasures, buried in secret, come forth now, in the name of Jesus. Yokes assigned to frustrate my efforts, break, in the name of Jesus. Where is the Lord God of Elijah, move me forward by fire, in the name of Jesus. Oil of favor from heaven, baptize my head, in the name of Jesus. Evil fingers pointed against my destiny, wither, in the name of Jesus. Any invisible chain on my legs, break, by the blood of Jesus and in the mighty name of the conquering KING, in the name of Jesus.

Anointing for victory laughter, fall upon my life, in the name of Jesus. Barriers and strongholds erected to stop me, scatter, in the name of Jesus. Anti-progress enchantments and divination, backfire, in the name of Jesus. Every power adding sluggishness to my breakthroughs, die, in the name of Jesus. My mouth, receive the anointing of the over comer, in the name of Jesus. Thou Great Physician, heal my root; Now in the powerful name of the undefeated one Jesus Christ.

Ancient gates, blocking my laughter, catch fire, in the name of Jesus. My Father, enlarge my coast to a dumbfounding degree, in the name of Jesus. My Father, my Father, pull darkness away from my environment, in the name of Jesus. Evil loads of my father's house, die, in the name of Jesus. Father, give me a glory that cannot be doubted.

In Jesus' name.

Amen

The Healing Decree

I cover myself and soak my mind, my blood, bones and flesh in the wonder working POWER, of the blood of Jesus. I barricade my body from every invasion by disease germs, in the name of Jesus. Holy Ghost fire, burn all disease deposits in my body to ashes, in the name of Jesus. Blood of Jesus, laminate my life, in the name of Jesus.

I silence the voice of sickness speaking against my life, in the name of Jesus. Let the blood of Jesus immunize me from every infirmity, in the name of Jesus. Anything I have eaten or swallowed, presently working against my health, be dissolved by the power of God, in the name of Jesus.

I decree that I shall not die. I empower my body to resist diseases! My body, resist and reject every killer disease, in the name of Jesus. I am healed today by the Power of God, the Son and the Holy Spirit in my Life!

Any organ in my body, performing below expectation, receive the resurrection power of the Lord Jesus Christ, in the name of Jesus. I shall not die but live to declare the works of God, in the name of Jesus. All arrows of infirmity, fired against me, go back to the sender, in the name of Jesus. Thou power of the wasters, my body is not your victim, clear away, in the name of Jesus.

Any curse of infirmity, working against me, die, in the name of Jesus. Any ladder or pipe supplying evil current into my body, break away, in the name of Jesus. I receive divine tonic and vitamins by the power in the blood of Jesus. My immune system, become unchallengeable by any infirmity, in the name of Jesus.

Yokes and covenants of diseases, break, in the name of Jesus. Any program of the spirit of death for my body, be extinguished, in the name of Jesus. Witchcraft sponsored infirmity will not come close to my camp, in the name of Jesus. I speak woe unto every troublers of the Israel of my life, in the name of Jesus.

I arrest any serpent of infirmity troubling my body, in the name of Jesus. Destructive infirmities, hear the word of the Lord, die, in the name of Jesus. I cut off the tentacles of internal disease spreading in my body, in the name of Jesus. Power base of infirmity, dry up and die, in the name of Jesus. Health arresters, be arrested by fire.

Holy Ghost fire, melt away every infirmity in my body organs. I fire back every arrow of affliction tormenting my body, in the name of Jesus. I kill and decree that every killer disease die and pass out of my body now, by the power of God who created me. Come out by bowel expel in ease and be gone forever, now by fire, in the blood of Jesus.

The battle of the terrible and the mighty against my health, expire, in the name of Jesus. Thou great physician, Jesus Christ, heal me now. Yokes of infirmity, break into pieces, in the name of Jesus. Authority of infirmity scorpions over my life, terminate, in the name of Jesus.

Every cell in my body, hear the word of the Lord, reject evil commands, in the name of Jesus. Let my bodily organs become too hot for any disease to handle, in the name of Jesus. I charge my body with the fire of the Holy Ghost, in the name of Jesus. Blood of Jesus, sanitize my body and make me whole.

In the name of Jesus

Amen

Prayer to Invoke My Angelic Benefits: Blessings

Angels come alive today on my behalf, run to rescue my wealth, prosperity, riches, and health and bring all good things to me today.

I refuse to allow my angels of blessings to depart before releasing my covenant and authorized blessings to my atmosphere and my presence. In the name of Jesus.

O Lord, promote and advance me. In the name of Jesus.

O Lord, transport me from minimum to maximum.

O Lord, touch me with your unchanging hand, and allow my angels to show me the way to your divine destiny for my life. In Jesus name.

O Lord, allow my angels who hear all conversations about me to convert my negatives to positives. In Jesus name.

I release the angels assigned to my success, to use the Blood of Jesus and the Axe of Fire, to cut off all dead links to the idol of my father's house and dead work that will not ensure my foot path to success. In Jesus name.

By the power in the blood of Jesus, I arise from fear to faith.

My angels align me with faith talkers of the same destiny. In the name of Jesus.

My angels will cause me to I receive restoration for what I lost through unbelief, in the name of Jesus.

O Lord, make my angels a source of blessings to me and me a source of blessing to others. In the name of Jesus.

My Father, arise and do what is necessary to cause my angels to bring revival to my life. In the name of Jesus.

Every chained spirit and chained blessing, I command my angels through the power of Jesus Christ to cause them to be released by fire. In the name of Jesus.

I stand in agreement with my angels, who are working for me and with men, for a great expected end of BLESSINGS!

That all idle works and word, concerning me, will die.

In the name of Jesus.

AMEN

Chief Apostle Dr. J. G. Rice

Prayer to Invoke My Angelic Benefits: Deliverance

I use the blood of Jesus to allow my angels to cancel every ordination of paralysis and death, in the name of Jesus.

Any and all problems attached to my name, my angels will kill and cause to die NOW, in Jesus name.

My angels will cause confusion and break up all strange meetings held about me and against my destiny, in the name of Jesus.

My angels will show me my enemies afar off. My angels have been released now to stand against faith destroyers, in the name of Jesus.

I decree my angels have been assigned, O Lord, to deliver me from any stronghold Satan may have in my life because of my sins and those of my ancestors, in Jesus' name.

Angels you are released to break all known and unknown bondage in my life with the blood of Jesus.

Angels you will turn me from trouble with any past soul ties.

I break all ungodly soul ties with all sex partners of the past, in the name of Jesus.

Father, let the angels place Godly hedges of thorns to surround me and my family from all hurt, harm, and danger, in the name of Jesus.

Let the angels of God pursue all my pursuers to surrender, in the name of Jesus.

My angels today will cancel all known and unknown curses and nullify their consequences upon my life, in Jesus' name.

My Father, give my angels the power to face all the challenges of the enemy and to overcome them, in the name of Jesus.

My angels will not allow to be loosed on myself the bondage and torment of fear, in the name of Jesus.

Angel of God blow fire, and let every tree planted by fear in my life dry to the roots.

In the name of Jesus

AMEN

Prayer to Invoke My Angelic Benefits: Promotion

Angel of the Lord, provide the way for me to see and understand, as you lead me into divine promotion today, in the name of Jesus.

Lord, make me succeed and bring me into abundant prosperity, in the name of Jesus.

As you release my angels to war on my behalf and to provide insight on my wealthy place.

I see, with the anointing, what my angels are speaking to me today. Promotion, progress and success, arise and locate my destiny by fire, in the name of Jesus.

Spirit of sluggishness, loose your hold upon my angels and my life and die, in the name of Jesus.

Spirit of Fear and storm of panic, depart from my life by fire, in the name of Jesus.

Let the blood of Jesus cleanse me, from head to toe, from every evil mark, in the name of Jesus.

My Father, let my heavens open so my angels will be released to evoke power to my life, in the name of Jesus.

You windows of heaven, open for my destiny by fire and the hand of my angels, in the name of Jesus.

Special anointing to pray above my normal level, come upon my life now, in the name of Jesus!

Ancestral family curses, break, by the power in the blood of Jesus.

O Lord, let everything that needs replacement in my life be replaced, so that my angels can have free reign to bless me and my family. In the name of Jesus.

Lord Jesus, pump your blood into my body. In the name of Jesus.

Angels make me to hear the sound of Laughter in my bones.

Fight against any demonic gang planning to steal my laughter, be disgraced, in the name of Jesus.

O God, arise and visit my life with permanent blessings, brought by your spirit and my angels, in the name of Jesus.

Father, give me a victory that cannot be disputed, in the name of Jesus.

AMEN

Prayer to Invoke My Angelic Benefits: Protection

I declare and I decree, my life shall not be disgraced by the gates of hell, in the name of Jesus.

My angels shall not let me dash my foot against a stone.

My angels shall protect my property and my beings from this time on.

My enemy will see my Angel of Protection is with me and flea from my presence.

My angel shall attend secret meetings and reveal to me the plan of the enemy towards me, and provide a way of escape for me.

O God, arise and dig the grave of my "Hamaan" and plan my testimony of SUCCESS in the name of Jesus.

I shall not miss my angel unaware, in the name of Jesus.

I break every unconscious agreement with the enemy, in the enemy, in the name of Jesus.

Dark powers of corrupt and envious people over my life, die and be exposed by my angel, in the name of Jesus.

My Warring Angel shall destroy back-up powers and dry up replacement powers of the enemy, in the name of Jesus.

I grant permission to my angels to work on my behalf and defeat with me demonic assignments as I sleep, eat, rise, walk, pray, and praise God!

I cancel every astral assignment over my life, in the name of Jesus.

O God, arise and banish all the forces of evil from me.

Reveal to my angels and assign them to destroy the powers of darkness that may be rounded up against me.

Empower them to win the battles for me Father I pray and decree, in the name of Jesus.

My angel shall prevent me from the polygamous curses troubling my life, in the name of Jesus.

My angel, I decree, shall cut off the horns of the wicked power by the power in the blood of Jesus.

My angel shall defeat every serpent programming disgrace against me

My angel will cut off your head, in the name of Jesus.

My angel will reveal and defeat every satanic altar in heaven and earth bearing my name, and cause it to catch fire, in the name of Jesus.

My angels will go into the heavens and cut off Powers planting curses in my star, making then die, in the name of Jesus.

I decree my angel will release my star, NOW, from voodoo or fetish powers, in the name of Jesus.

O God, arise and release my angels to unblock my blessings.

In the name of Jesus

AMEN

Prayers to Invoke My Angelic Benefits: Waging War Against the Enemy

My angels are released from God to take vengeance against my enemies.

They will release the ten plagues of Egypt upon every coven troubling my life.

Against every person speaking evil against my life as soon as the words are spoken against me.

In the name of Jesus.

I decree every unused angel of the Lord to be on my side to bring blessings to me at every opportunity.

I decree every unused or unoccupied angel to be at my defense, now and forevermore,

I decree every un-commanded angel to post themselves at war against those who war against me from now on.

Woe unto every power assigned to stagnate me.

My angels are assigned against you.

In the name of Jesus.

Let the candle of the wicked be put out by my angel.

In the name of Jesus.

O God, distribute sorrow to all covens assigned against me.

In the name of Jesus.

O God arise, let your anger be released through your hand and commanded by my angels.

Breakfast, lunch and dinners of sorrow to any power hired to curse me.

In the name of Jesus.

I release catastrophe, by the hand of the almighty Angels of God, and poverty upon any power assigned to rubbish my destiny.

In the name of Jesus.

Ancestral debt collectors, angels loose their paper work and loose their hold.

In the name of Jesus.

Let desolation and destruction pursue my pursers.

In the name of Jesus.

Every voice releasing instructions to torment and hinder my life, die,.

In the name of Jesus.

Warrior angels from heaven, arise, lock up every satanic high priest troubling my life.

In the name of Jesus.

Negative powers assigned to redesign my destiny, die.

In the name of Jesus.

Every power mocking my God, die.

Every power challenging my destiny, die.

Power of repeated problems, die.

In the name of Jesus

AMEN

Prayers to Invoke My Angelic Benefits: Dislodge Evil

Lord, let my words matter in heaven.

In Jesus name.

Let my angels bring you my praises

and may you receive them into your bosom.

O Lord, promote my angels

to fight in the heavenlies with this prayer

In the name of Jesus.

All the forces of evil,

may my angels stone your foreheads.

In the name of Jesus.

O Lord, let the stars of angelic hosts

fight against every witchcraft bird assigned against me.

In the name of Jesus.

Let the sword of the Lord, by the hand of my Angels,

arise and dislodge every evil program in the heavens.

In the name of Jesus.

Any power opposing the purpose of God for my life,

my angels will misguide and destroy you.

May you be shifted away.

In the name of Jesus

AMEN

Prayers to Invoke My Angelic Benefits: Dismantle Evil Agendas

All satanic investments, be shaken out of the heavenlies, in the name of Jesus.

Let every power opposing the prophetic agenda for my life be dismantled, by the hand of my angels, who will see your plan burned by the fire of God. In the name of Jesus.

I prophesy over my life, that my angles will wake up NOW, from my voice and by my name, (mention your name), Wake up! In the name of Jesus.

I decree my angels will shake off every agenda of bewitchment. Be shaken off, NOW! In the name of Jesus.

I pull down every dominion in the heavenlies working against me. In the name of Jesus.

Father God , let the sun and moon expel all evil plantations against me,. In the name of Jesus.

Angels command and let the stars fight against my enemies. In the name of Jesus.

O Lord, allow my Covenant Angels to subdue kings, peoples, sorceries, and enchantments, for my sake. In the name of Jesus.

Every horn of darkness planning to scatter my life, scatter. In the name of Jesus.

O Lord, maximize your altar in my life. In the name of Jesus.

My Angel of Peace will now I scatter every evil confrontation sent my way to upset my day and my vision of peace. In the name of Jesus.

Anything in my life, that is making the enemy to ask where is my God, my angels will show up and show them the God of my salvation, whom will answer by fire.

I then shall receive divine solution. In the name of Jesus.

Oh Lord, allow my angels to set a remembrance for me and my family.

In the name of Jesus

AMEN

Prayers to Invoke My Angelic Benefits: Dismantling by Fire

Every altar mounted against my destiny, allow my Angel of Flaming Fire to dismantle, NOW, in the heavenlies. Be dismantled and utterly destroyed NOW, in the name of Jesus.

The shadow of my background will not cut me off. My angels will unplug and undo any unfavorable report concerning me, in the name of Jesus.

O Lord, allow my angels to see a path and re-open my life unto breakthroughs, in the name of Jesus.

O Lord, allow my angels to silence every accusation in the heavenlies against me while I sleep. Cause them to forever be broken, in the name of Jesus.

O Lord, let my angels prevent me from eating or drinking anything unhealthy, deadly or that will cause me to be sick.

My healer Jesus, please purge sickness out of my life, in the name of Jesus. The devil will not bury me through poison, in the name of Jesus.

My angels will throw over and spill ever vial of death concerning me, and it will run back to the enemy who sent it and pour into their pores, in the name of Jesus.

My angels and I, through agreement, paralyze every activity of wickedness in the heavenlies against me, in the name of Jesus.

My angels will clear the records and render Satan and his informants nullified. Every satanic information registered in the heavenlies against me, be nullified, in the name of Jesus.

I command all the days and nights left in this year, that my angels will cause them to bring me favor and blessings through this decree:

Angels, I decree you to bring favor to and in my life NOW, in the name of Jesus.

Angels, you will remind the sun that it will not smite me by day, nor the moon by night. Instead, they will arise and fight for me in this season, and forever more.

AMEN

I Release the Spirit of Rest and Peace On My Journey

Every power assigned to turn my glory to shame, and to cause unrest my future, die, in the name of Jesus.. Any poison in my body, die, in the name of Jesus. Ancient gates, blocking my joy, catch fire, in the name of Jesus.

O heavens, lift up your sword, slay all spirit husbands/wives, in the name of Jesus. Any problem in my life caused by using my hair as a baby, or as an adult, Any trips to persons seeking others to speak curses against me , BOOMARANG to the sender with triple the amount of said words.

May those words spoken over my life, by the enchanter die, May they be fearful to re-utter them against me, in the name of Jesus. May they reverse the curse from me to the sender in agreement as to not temp the Lord my God! Dark powers supervising my problems, loose your hold and return to the sender to trouble me no more. Die toward me and my future, and my generations in the name of Jesus.

Powers planted in my childhood to trouble my future, hear the word of the Lord, die, in the name of Jesus. I will have and now evoke the spirit of peace and restfulness in joy. Every Lizard, Python, or Dragon spirit loosed at the root of my foundation and dwelling place, I Mortify you by the power of Jesus, Blood up and scatter never to return to me, find the sender and abide, without access to return. In Jesus name, Every Dust, Potion, Oil, or Liquid, sprinkled, or shook against me "Die" in Jesus name.

Every form of evil spoken against my marriage, bed of marriage, and future of marriage DIE NOW, Burn by fire, ash away, and blow away in Jesus name. I decree that no BITES, HOT LASHES, or Marks on my body will appear and disappear, die, in the name of Jesus.

My seasons and times are in the will of the Father which has given me the authority to "HAVE ("ZOE") life, and LIFE MORE ABUNDANTLY". Therefore in the Name of Jesus I Decree, and Declare that I will Thrive, Survive , and have good success. I decree that My Father, God the King of Kings will let my past maximum become my minimum, of Failures, my Happiness explode, and my laughter rise, in the name of Jesus. Today, I set aside any evil contention, I purpose not to strive against mankind in the name of Jesus. Every distance stolen from my life by the enemy, I repossess you Now in the Favor of God.

I declare...

This year, like a clay in the hands of the potter, the Lord will make what He wants out of my life, in the name of Jesus.

This year, the Lord will do with me whatever He wants, in the name of Jesus.

This year, the Lord will make me the head and not tail.

This year, every snare of the fowler assigned against me shall perish.

This year, I render the habitation of darkness assigned against me desolate,.

This year, divine deposits shall settle in my life,.

This year, I enter into the covenant of favor.

This year, the anointing of success and fruitfulness shall rest on me.

This year, I will not be a candidate of sweating without result, in Jesus' name.

This year, all obstacles on my way of progress shall be dismantled.

This year, my God shall arise and my stubborn pursuers shall scatter.

This year, those that mock me in the past shall celebrate with me.

This year, my Goliath, my Absalom, and my Joab, shall experience destruction.

This year, every power assigned to cut short my life shall die.

This year, my prayers shall always provoke angelic violence for my good.

This year, I shall speak and my words shall bring testimonies.

Every evil tree planted against my freedom, die, in the name of Jesus. I prophesy deliverance and freedom upon my life, in the name of Jesus. Every pin that is stuck in a "doll" bearing my name or destiny" will return to the sender.

The doll of ill wishes and diabolical attachments shall be disannulled from my life. It shall catch fire, but I shall live and not be burnt or hurt. It shall return to the sender to come again no more. Defeated by the blood of JESUS. I will not feel the effects of such works but they will be returned to the head of the sender, In Jesus name.

This year and forever more, as I am a Child of the Great I am Jehovah, the enemy will see me as a child of God the Father. Therefore the sorcerer, witch or warlock, will not accept any assignment concerning me and will see the angels of the Lord fighting on my behalf when they try to glimpse in my future and refuse Payment, or bribery to try to even ensue works against t me. They will refuse and not take any evil assignment concerning me.

This year these effect shall not render my ministry or my members void of substance, faith, finances or attendance. The meanderings of the enemy will not prosper in my destiny, in the name of Jesus. Let the excesses of darkness upon my destiny be checked by fire, in the name of Jesus.

Every satanic hold up against my destiny, die, in the name of

Jesus.

Every conspiracy of darkness working against my destiny, die, in the name of Jesus.

I break the law of death over my life, in the name of Jesus.

Every covenant of death with this year, be broken, in the name of Jesus.

Every satanic prophesy over my destiny, be nullified by the power in the blood of Jesus.

Resurrection of affliction, die, in the name of Jesus.

By the blood of Jesus, I am invisible to aggressive elements, in the name of Jesus.

AMEN

The Resurrection Power Prayer

My portions and water shall be secured by the blood of Jesus, by my angels and by my faith. The Resurrection Power of Jesus remains on my Life, Therefore I will not be defeated in Jesus name. I do have the same RESURRECTION POWER as my Lord and Savior, Jesus the Christ! Therefore I decree I shall not be buried but I shall revive and resurrect!

I decree to the winds of Repeat destruction and failure. Thou evil power sponsoring repeated afflictions, die, in the name of Jesus. Holy Spirit increase my speed and my efforts in life, in the name of Jesus. Every magic in any house I have entered, be destroyed by fire, in the name of Jesus. Every evil power that has established evil authority in my family My family shall resurrect in their faith towards the living God.

We walk back into my childhood and correct my foundations, in the name of Jesus. Every satanic plantation planted in my childhood, be dissolved by the fire of the Holy Ghost, in the name of Jesus. Every effect of anything I have swallowed or eaten as a child, be nullified, in the name of Jesus.

Powers assigned to capture my star, loose your hold, in the name of Jesus.

Powers planted in my childhood, to trouble my future, hear the word of the Lord, the Lord will cause dryness to come upon you today, in the name of Jesus.

Powers planted in my childhood, to trouble my future, I dry up your river, even as Jordan was dried up, in the name of Jesus.

Powers planted in my childhood, to trouble my future, I dry up your roots even as the Lord dried up the fig tree, in the name of Jesus.

Powers planted in my childhood, to trouble my future, I knock down your gates, in the name of Jesus.

Powers planted in my life to trouble my future, I break in pieces your gates of brass, in Jesus' name.

Powers planted in my youth, to trouble my future, I cut in sunder the bras of iron, in the name of Jesus.

Powers planted in my teenage years, to trouble my future, I break down your walls, even as the walls of Jericho was broken down, in the name of Jesus.

Powers planted in my young adult to trouble my future, I cut off your cords, I cast them away, in Jesus' name.

Powers planted in my adult to trouble my future, I command you to bend your knee to Jesus.

Powers planted in my marriage, to trouble my future, I put a cord around your tongue, in the name of Jesus.

Powers planted in my child bearing, to trouble my future, I bore a thorn in your jaw, in the name of Jesus.

Powers planted in my education, to trouble my future, I take away your throne, in the name of Jesus.

Powers planted in my Spiritual Growth, to trouble my future, I command you to sit in the dust, in the name of Jesus.

I break all curses, sins, trespasses or iniquity coming down my family line, in the name of Jesus. I come in agreement with the Holy Spirit now the ruler of my thoughts and the teacher of my soul to destroy the spiritual embargo on my mother's side and on my father's side, ten generations backward, in the name of Jesus.,

Father, my God, the Great I Am, any covenant of the past that has been broken that would enrage you, our Forgiving God, to punish our generation, we repent. We ask for forgiveness and restoration back to the place of Rest and Restoration for you are now our God and we serve you in righteousness and peace, In Jesus name.

We renounce, and disconnect to . Any dark covenant with my place of birth, break, in the name of Jesus.

I make my Confession

I will not Struggle

I WILL subdue the Land peacefully

In Jesus Name

AMEN

The Prayer of Public Success

My Father, purge my blood line, in the name of Jesus. Pattern of darkness in my family line, break, in Jesus' name. What my father did not enjoy, I will enjoy it, in the name of Jesus. O God, backdate the blessings of my ancestors and give them to me, in the name of Jesus. I make a contrary declaration to that of the enemy, in the name of Jesus.

Let my destiny be re-arranged to favor my life, in the name of Jesus. I refuse to struggle for what my parents struggled with, in the name of Jesus. Breakthroughs of Spiritual miscarriages to Godly Seeds, die, in the name of Jesus. Evil cycles in my bloodline, die, in the name of Jesus.

The land has been given to me to possess. My enemies will hear the sound of the HORNETS and leave, NOW, in Jesus name. Whatever the enemy has set in motion, I reverse them, I put them in reverse gear, in the name of Jesus.

Let any reading materials coming down to me from generations let them, from them be filtered through the cross, in the name of Jesus.. I decree public success. I thank God for all the good news, publications, information and social printings in my favor and that promote my success.

Any dormant success I've inherited from my forefathers will be released unto me. I claim the good things and reject the evil, all old debts will be cancelled and my inheritance will come to me free and clear of debt in Jesus' name.

Those that hear my words publically will be drawn to be a blessing to my life from this day and forever more and will work towards my public success and my private victories.

I decree an army of people wanting to do me good, to rise to my defense and that the favor of God will bless their lives as they are a blessing to me. I command my success to flow unhindered in Jesus name.

Blood of Jesus, flow through my family history and wash away every ground of satanic attack against my destiny, in the name of Jesus.

AMEN

Confessions For My Bloodline As An Intercessor

My Father, I ask in repentance for forgiveness of all my family sins, in the name of Jesus. Every descending pattern that Satan uses to perpetuate his destruction on my family line, be wiped off by the blood of Jesus. Every power causing problem to escalate in my family line, die, in the name of Jesus. Thou power of destructive pattern and habit, be destroyed by the power in the blood of Jesus.

My Father, send your angels to bring each member of my family out of darkness into light, in the name of Jesus. O God arise and send Your warrior angels to do battle for my family, in the name of Jesus.

I bind every evil king reigning in my family with chain, in the name of Jesus. Sacrifices done on my behalf, unknown or know to me, caging in me from my root, die, in the name of Jesus.

Family spirits power and supervising powers in charge of my father's house, die, in the name of Jesus.. Foundational button, pressed against my advancements, die, in the name of Jesus. If there are any Strange animals rituals abiding or dormant in my roots, die, in the name of Jesus.

By the power in the blood of Jesus, we renounce the untrue gods that we have served, that has brought us into collective captivity, money, sex, fame, flesh, pride, and unstable emotions; in the name of Jesus. Thou power of collective demonization in my family line, I destroy you, in the name of Jesus.

Every satanic odors, or burning of candles, come out of the closet of my family, be exposed and burned up at the root in Jesus name, in the MIGHTY name of Jesus. Every curse under which my family labor, be broken by the power in the blood of Jesus

Every UNGODLY covenant under which my family labors, be broken by the power in the blood of Jesus. Dedications to evil or the underworld of darkness, that I have been rendered to against my will, that speaks against my family line and calls us to darkness, be broken, in the name of Jesus.

Every power altering the destiny of my family, be scattered, in the name of Jesus. Every affliction in my family line, die, in the name of Jesus. Every satanic investment, in the heavenlies, expected to manifest seasonal evil in my family, be crushed, in the name of Jesus. My Father, lay a new foundation for my family line, in the name of Jesus.

Every power of the wicked avenger upon my family line, be destroyed, in the name of Jesus. Blood of Jesus, neutralize any evil thing inherited from the blood of my parents, in the name.

I command the Resting of God of My Family and My Life as they are Children of God. I proclaim the Lord Jesus Christ as Lord over all the issues and affairs of my life, in the name of Jesus. I bind and reject every spirit of failure associated with my life, in the name of Jesus.

I bind and reject all evil companion spirits, in the name of Jesus. I bind and reject all carnal spirits, in the name of Jesus. I bind and reject all spirits of affliction, in the name of Jesus.

I bind and reject every evil monitoring spirit, in the name of Jesus. I break and dissolve every curse attached to my foundation, in the name of Jesus. I break the evil confidence of my enemies, in the name of Jesus.

Every dark power in possession of the keys to my breakthrough, fall down and die, in the name of Jesus. Every satanic altar assigned to my success in life, catch fire, in the name of Jesus.

O God arise and uproot anything You did not plant inside my life and my ministry now in Jesus name.

I decree it so, NOW, in my ministry today.

In Jesus name

AMEN

Prayer of Spiritual Renewal and Restoration

Jesus the Christ, Son of the Living God, plug my prayer life into the socket of the Holy Ghost, therefore, let the current of holiness and power flow through my life now by fire! in Jesus' name. Every power draining the Godly virtues of my life, expire and die by fire! in the name of Jesus.

Holy Spirit, renew my spirit-man and restore unto me the joy of my salvation in the name of Jesus. Holy Spirit make me hunger and thirst for your righteousness in the name of Jesus.

Fire of resurrection, ENTER into my life now and let that fire propel me throughout this year and forever! In the name of Jesus.

I plug my prayer altar to God's power of signs and wonders, in the name of Jesus. Let the electric current of the Holy Ghost electrocute every satanic agent playing with my life in Jesus' name.

Every dead area of my prayer life, every dead area of my daily devotion and communion with God, every dead area of my bible-reading and study, hear the Voice of Resurrection: COME ALIVE NOW and FLOURISH BY FIRE! In the name of Jesus.

Spirit of Death and Hell, my life is not your candidate this year, therefore, VANISH BY FIRE from my destiny and family! In the name of Jesus. Fire of revival, ravage every spiritual coldness in my life today and forever, In the name of Jesus.

Arrows of worry, discouragement, inadequacy, depression, frustration, skepticism and weariness fired against my life, gather yourselves together and GO BACK to your sender!!! in the name of Jesus.

Every power assigned to make me stagger and fall-away from faith this year, you are a LIAR! Somersault and die! In Jesus name.

Holy Spirit, inoculate me with the full blast of your power, in the name of Jesus

I receive my family to be restored to you, Father God, in Jesus name.

AMEN

NOTES

Section 4
"Special Forces Prayers"
Of
Deliverance
Power
and
Victory

NOTES

Section 4

"Special Forces Prayers"

Of Deliverance

Power and Victory

Alerting My Morning and Taking Captive My Day	Page 177
Back To God Prayer	Page 185
Spiritual Warfare Prayer	Page 191
Prayer for My Leaders and the World	Page 193
I Am Chief Apostle, and this is a time of Prayer	Page 195
I Decree I Have Favor	Page 201
We Decree We Will Come Back To God Prayer	Page 203
Prayer of Thanksgiving	Page 209
Set Us Free and Give Us the Bondage Releasing Anointing	Page 210
Prayer of Evangelism	Page 212
Oh God, Save Them Prayer	Page 214
Prayer for Those In Need of Salvation	Page 225
Rebuking the Curse Off Our Families Finances	Page 222
Prayer of Repentance	Page 225
Breaking the Back of the Enemy	Page 230
Prayer for the Author	Page 233

NOTES

Alerting My Morning and Taking Captive My Day

God, I thank you this morning as I alert my morning and take captive my day according to your word. I thank you Father that the cares of yesterday have passed and gone. I thank you Lord that the corruption of yesterday did not follow me into a new day. I thank you Lord that the sickness and disease of yesterday has been defeated, and that I walk in victory this morning. I thank you Lord because you said that I could rejoice in you, because this is a new day and your mercies are new this morning. Favor is new this morning! Expectations are new today!

So I alert the morning in my life, and I take captive my day, to line up with your word. Angels, that even may have slept last night, wake up and be about the Fathers bidding concerning me. Bring me blessings, bring me the wealth of the gentile, and bring me the inheritance of those that despitefully use me. According to the word of God, I set my mind to be used today for kingdom assignment. I set my heart today to be used for kingdom assignment. I set my thought pattern to line up with the Word of God. I set even the sepulcher of our throat to speak of the goodness and glory of God. For Lord you are good and your mercies endure forever. Let now the children of the most high God say, "Lord you're good and your mercies endure forever." Let those that name the name of Jesus Christ as Lord and savior now decree, Lord you are good and your mercies endure forever.

God I thank you that as I abide in you, that you abide in me. You said, seek first the kingdom and everything else will be added to us, so Lord I am abiding in your word. I'm holding fast to your teachings and I'm living in accordance with them. It is my desire today to be your true disciples.

I am abiding in and united to your vine for I cannot bear forth fruit unless I abide in you. So father, I abide in you, right now. Give me an Abiding Spirit in you, Father, for you are the vine and we are the branches living in you. Therefore I decree I will bring forth abundant fruit, much fruit, that will not wither. I will be that voice for you today, of evangelism, that will cause someone to be saved. That will cause someone to be changed and receive the power of the Holy Spirit.

Father I thank you that I am not cut off from you, but that I am united with you. I realize that I cannot do anything without Jesus, your son. So God I ask that the spirit of the living God, by the way of the Father, the Son and the Holy Spirit, come and live in my life, that my words will remain in you and continue to live in my heart. And God, whatever I ask you said you would do it for me, according to your word. I stand on St John 15:7 today, because I purpose, yes I purpose to seek first the kingdom and have everything else added to me.

I declare that my day will line up with your divine connections. I declare that my day will go on purpose and provision, that I will be where I am supposed to be and meet who I am supposed to meet and see who I am supposed to see, by the divine cosmetic and cosmos clap of the Holy Spirit and the universe that you have destined us to abide in until your coming. Your coming will bring us into the revealed word, truth, love, destiny, prosperity, and kingdom connections!

Thank you father that my connections will continue to produce fruit. Father I am honored that you chose me to be saved, so God I honor and glorify you by your grace and show myself approved, walking worthy of our calling today, in the name of Jesus. Lord I love you, I abide in that love today, in the name of Jesus. You have assured me, according to your word, that if I continue in your instructions that you will bless me. That if I keep an Obedient Spirit, you will bless me with a Teachable Spirit So God I command my day to be one that's obedient to your word, your power and direction, in Christ Jesus. I am a part of the promise, the body of Christ, and we pray unity of the 120, for myself and others.

I will not compromise the word. I will not compromise the Spirit of Truth, but I will speak the truth in love. Father you said that if we will speak the truth that our joy might be filled lord, and as our joy is filled our strength is made strong in you, for the joy of the lord is our strength. Send me the Spirit of Joy and Delight today. Send me a Spirit of Happiness today. Send me the Spirit of Completion and Overflowing Joy today, for I walk in abundance and live in the overflow today. Men shall give to my bosom from the North, South, East and West today. Blessing shall come to me from the North, South, East and West today. Good health shall abide with me from the North, South, East and West. It is from the abundance of the Spirit of the Living God that my health springs forth like the oasis in the midst of the desert.

Thank you lord for the mountain of praise, the mountain of Zion, that is in my life. Thank you lord for the mountain of Hebron that is in my life. Thank you Lord for every stone that has been set as a memorial to the things you have brought me through Lord, that I can look upon those stones and know that this is a testimony! I know that as you have done it before, you shall and will do it again. Father I thank you for your word today, it is the truth that makes me free because I am a born and begotten child of you God. So I will not, I do not, I shall not deliberately, knowingly or habitually practice sin, for your nature abides in us today, your principles of light remains permanently within us.

I will not yield my flesh to sin. I will not yield my spirit to sin, but I will command it to line up with your word. Let truth abide in me God, that I will direct my own selfish ways to come in line with you. Help me not to be self-centered, but to do what your kingdom needs first. Help me to grow and not to be stagnant. I receive the

Spirit of Growth in my life.

Lord I thank you that through my faith, you dwell and settle down in my heart. So therefore I become mature in you, I become perfected in your love, I become perfected in your grace and glory, I become a devoted follower that experiences life everlasting and fullness of glory. Thank you that I will have joy today, I will laugh, I will love, and I will embrace today. I know today that you are the King of King and Lord of Lord in my life. Thank you for being sovereign over me.

Thank you for providing for me on today, with the power to alert my morning and take captive my day. I pray, in the name of Jesus, that I might know this love that surpasses my knowledge. That it will go deep into the depths of my spirit, deep into the depths of my heart, deep into the depths of my understanding that I might be filled with all measure of your fullness God. Grow up in me today! Oh my God, be bigger in me today then you were yesterday. Let life change God, let me know that you are in me Lord. I pray today that I will be that Evangelist that you have called all of us to be, that we would have soul winning on our mind. That I would not be selfish with my salvation, but would share to the left and to the right in front of us and behind us, with whomever we come in contact with. That I will open the doors of their heart so that your words would not go in vain or void, but that they would accomplish what they set out to do because they will be your words God. Teach us how to minister with compassion, because you moved with compassion and healing came forth

God I thank you for healing. I thank you for the Spirit of Healing that's in my life. I thank you Lord that as I speak your word today, the Spirit of Compassion and Healing will come forth. I thank you Lord that I can speak it with revelation. I will speak it with manifestation and with the joy of hope, that there is still hope in Jesus. I release my morning, my day today, to be under the Glory of Jesus. I release Jesus Christ to be full in me. I release the glory to glow in my life, to give permission to the Holy Spirit to shine in me today, and to teach me something new in the word of God that I might be better because of a relationship with you father and having the holy spirit in my life. Son of the living God, rise up big in me today, stretch yourself forth in me, anoint me afresh in the mighty name of Jesus. Send forth your latter rain in my life, don't let me be dry and dusty Father, but I receive the rain of the lord in my life.

I thank you Lord that the seeds of goodness that have been planted in me is springing forth. I don't just have mustard seed faith, but a mustard tree faith. Thank you Lord that I am growing, my branches are becoming strong, I have the power to reproduce, and I reproduce after my own kind daily. I seek for someone to come into the kingdom daily. Today is the day that the Lord has made and I rejoice and am glad in it. I do know that you're good because I've tasted of you, and God, today is a good day. Today is a mighty day! Today is an awesome day! Somebody will bless me today!

I will find a desire of my heart today that will come forth and make me smile. Somebody will say a kind word to me today. I will be friendly to someone today, and the Spirit of Friendliness will reproduce itself in my life. I'm going to be helpful to someone today, and the Spirit of Helpfulness will reproduce in my life 100 fold. I'm will have the Spirit of Blessing upon my life and others, and the Spirit of Blessing is will reproduce itself in me. Today is a day of blessing, today is a day of hope. My hope is built in nothing less than Jesus' blood and righteousness, and so in the righteousness of God I set my hope today.

I bind the Spirit of Confusion away from me. I bind the Spirit of Cantankerous away from me. I bind the Spirit of Stinginess away from me. I bind the Spirit of Self-will away from me. I bind the Spirit of Idolatry away from me. I bind the Spirit of Gluttony away from me. Father, great deliver, I bind the Spirit of Argumentativeness, Strife, and Confusion away from me and I receive the Spirit of Righteousness and Joy! SHALOM PEACE! Abide over me today, now and forevermore.

As I alert my morning and I take captive my day, I receive the double portion of the Spirit of Peace. I speak again from the four winds, shalom over my day today. I speak shalom over everyone that I will come in contact with. That they will bring a Spirit of Peace into my environment, and my Spirit of Peace will connect with their Spirit of Peace, and the peace of God may abide. I decree that even if they are not saved, they will still have a peaceable spirit concerning me. I decree, Glorious Father, that they will want to bless me, even if there's a charge involved I will be shown favor. They will overreach to bless me and tell me to keep the abundance. I will see your hand in every area of my life today.

I will see discounts on my life today. My tithes shall activate themselves to bring me wealth and favor. Wherever I go to purchase something it will have a discount, it will be reduced ridiculously and even free. Because I am free in you, therefore free things come to me. Good things, quality things will cost me less, but I get more, in the name of Jesus. I decree favor with those landlords, keepers of my mortgage, banks and owners. Rulers over my residential domain, whether by rental or mortgage, I will have favor with them. I decree monthly reductions and payments of relief will come to my door. I will find rest in the land for with you have provided unto me. I decree today that my bills are paid. I decree that I am debt free today. I decree that the wealth of the heathens is laid up for me today. I decree that the heavens open up and pour me out good favor today. I decree that the Glory of God is on me today. I decree that the YES of the Holy Spirit is in my life today.

I decree that I will not make wrong turns or bad decisions, because the Holy Spirit will not lead me into error. So I lean my ear to hear of the Lord today. I lean my ear to hear what the Father is saying today, and I will listen to the Glory of God that's in my life today.

I will listen to the purpose of God in my life today. I will listen to what God has designed for me today. I will listen and decree that God has already orchestrated my life today. So I decree from Jeremiah, that my purpose is already been assigned. That there is no failure in me today and that it is already done, in the name of Jesus. I decree that God has already done everything and has laid it out, all I have to do is rejoice, pray, and be in place. Any distractions that will keep me out of place today, I cancel the assignment, in the name of Jesus.

I glorify God today because of who He is. My Father, the maker and creator of us all, Jehovah, the Great I Am, Father of Abraham, Isaac and Jacob, the Father of Jesus Christ of Nazareth, my Lord and Savior, ruler of heaven, earth and the universe, and the one who directs, fills and provides for me. The father of I magnify God today because of what He is. I cast my cares on Him today because He has already fixed it. Anything that comes my way, I am more than equipped to handle it with the glory and the anointing of God that is on my life. Any person that will come my way that needs a ready answer from God, I am already ready and equipped to give a right word of love, in the name of Jesus. Any down trodden spirit that will come my way, I've already sanctified myself with the hope of joy.

I will not be affected by negative behavior. I will not have my spirit turned by negative behavior. I will not have my spirit infiltrated by negative behavior. Instead I will stand under the blood of Jesus. I will stand under the covenant of Jesus. I will stand under the glory of Jesus. I will stand under the joy of Jesus. I will stand under the purpose of Jesus. I will stand under the anointing of Jesus. I have been equipped today. I have been set free today, therefore bondages have no business trying to come against me. I come against bondage. I come against fear. I come against the flesh of my mind that would lead me to remember who I use to be. I cancel that assignment, and my vision is set towards who God has assigned me to be today.

Today I alert my morning of blessing! Wake up and provide for me daily! I take captive my day! I seize this day for Gods Glory and notify my atmosphere to the wealth and health that we shall possess. My day, my week, my month, my year, my season, must release it NOW, on my behalf and in my favor! I reserve and preserve my days for prosperity. My times and seasons are happy, wealthy, healthy, and wise and sealed by the blood of Jesus. In the glorious , mighty name of Jesus Christ of Nazareth, son of the Living God, Jehovah Jireh.

AMEN

Back To God Prayer

Oh God, we glorify your name. We bow down before you God, we ask that you here us being needed for your spirit right now. Be merciful to us Lord, for we cry unto you daily. Oh God rejoice in the soul of your servant, for unto thee Lord do I lift up my soul, for thou Oh Lord are good and ready to forgive. You are plenteous and mercy to all those that call unto you. Give ear, oh God, to our prayers. Lord attend to the voice of our supplication. Lord we call on you now, so in the day of trouble when we call unto you, you will answer us.

Lord we realize there's none like you God. Neither are there any works like your works, for all nations whom you have made shall come and worship you. Oh Lord, Hallelujah Jesus, Hallelujah Jesus. We come and worship you, for you are great and you do wondrous things. We ask you to teach us your way, that we may walk in your truth. Unite our hearts to fear your name, oh God. We will praise you, oh our God, with all our hearts we will glorify your name. Lord we glorify your name forever more, for great are your mercy toward us, you delivered our soul from the lowest of hell.

Oh God the pride might even try to rise up against us, and even the assembly of the violent people may seek after us, but God you will not set us before them, for you are full of compassion, you are gracious, long-suffering, patience, and truth. So turn unto us oh God and have mercy unto us, give us strength. Lord give strength to your servants, save your handmaiden, In the name of Jesus. Save your male children, In the name of Jesus.

Show us a token for good that those that hate us may see us rise, and the presence of you God they will not be ashamed and we will not be ashamed, because you have helped us God,. You have comforted us. You are the foundation of our sanctification. You are the foundation of our destination. You are the right and ready just God. Oh God you are the hope of our hope. Set us free even in the pits of our mind. You set us free even in the pits of our emotions. You have called us to the altar for this time of prayer.

Oh God we lower ourselves before you. Oh God we debased ourselves that you may exalt us. Glorious is your name, oh God in the mighty name of Jesus. Oh God we call on Mount Zion night and day, that you might be able to console us, even in the midst of our entire situation. We thank you God, because you have established us, in the name of Jesus. We call forth the singers and the worshippers right now. Oh God, that we might sing a new song to the God of our salvation, in the name of Jesus.

Oh Lord all night and all day we cry before thee. Our prayers come before you God, we ask that you hear our cry. Oh God, you free us from among the dead, in the name of Jesus. You free us from Lying Spirits. You free us from doubt and unbelief. You free us from those things that are hopeless. Every grave clothes, we ask that you shake it off NOW, in the mighty name of Jesus. Oh God, we don't have any help other than you God.

From the north and south we cry unto you. We are broken Father, but yet we are whole because of your blood. So we ask you God our lover and our friend to be a gate around us, to compass all around us, to keep our soul from affliction, in the might name of Jesus. Wondrous works be known unto us. Show your loving kindness God. Show your faithfulness. Show your wondrous works towards us, in the mighty name of Jesus. We ask you now God, even as we ask you to come into our hearts, come into our mind and encompass us to the more God. For you are great and greatly to be praised. You are great and greatly to be feared. You are great and the Assembly of God to be reverence. And God we reverence your holy name, for your seed you have established forever.

You build up a throne and all generation. You made a covenant with us, even as you have done with our father Abraham, and our father David, and our father Isaac, and our father Jacob. Oh God you a covenant keeper and the midst of it all God. You a covenant keeper, you a mind regulator, we give your name praise, you beat down our foes before our face, and you send plague to take them away from us. You run our foes to the river and there they loose, because you allow that same river to encompass them, that you don't allow them to encompass us.

Oh God, in the might name of Jesus. We thank you for your glory, for you have made your glory to come all around us. We thank you God, you broke down all the hedges, and all the strong holds. You make void the covenant of the un-faithful, but with us God you established a covenant forever. We thank you God for the first fruit, bringing you the first praise, giving you the first born, giving you the first offering, giving the first of everything. We wake up, we acknowledge you in all our ways and you direct our paths. You've been our dwelling path in all generation, before the mountains where brought forth, before you formed the earth, and the world, from everlasting to everlasting you are God. We thank you God that trouble don't last always.

In the morning the joy comes. In the morning the faithfulness of your word return unto us in the morning. We thank you Lord, for we know the power of you. So teach us to number our days, that we may apply our hearts to wisdom. Satisfy us early with your mercy that we may rejoice all our days. Thank you now for the angels that you give charge over us.

Thank you now God, we abide under the shadow of the almighty, as we dwell in the secret place of the most high. We will say of you that you are our fortress, you are our refuge. We can say that we trust in you God. We can say that you delivered us from the fowler, from the noisome pestilence, that you cover us with your feathers, you cover us under your wings, and we trust in you. You are our shield and you are our buckler, in the name of Jesus.

We trust in you God, there's no evil that cometh our way, no evil shall befall us, no plague shall come nigh our dwelling. You given these angels charge over us, to keep us we will not dash our hand or foot against a stone. We will trample upon the lion. We will trample upon the dragon, and we will trample them under our feet, in the mighty name of Jesus. Because you set your love on us, there-fore God you deliver us, because you set us on high. I thank you Lord, you said we can call on your name and you will answer us. You said you satisfy us with long life, thank you Lord for long life, thank you Lord for long prosperous life.

Thank you Lord we give thanks unto you, it's a good thing to give thanks unto you Lord. Yes lord we sing praises unto your name for you've shown forth your loving kindness, even in the morning you've been faithful to us God, even in the night, so we give your name praise. With our hands we clap them and make glad, even with our voice we lift it up and say thank you. We lift our voice like a unicorn horn and you anoint us with fresh oil. We give you glory, we shall see our desires come to pass in our life.

Yes Lord we shall flourish, because we are planted in the courts of God. Thank you Lord we still bring forth fruit in old age. We will be fat and will flourish. We will be faithful, available, and teachable, and will flourish, and we will show that the Lord is

upright. He is my rock, there is no unrighteousness in you Lord. You made me glad; I triumph in your works. You made me glad; I triumph in the works of your hands.

Oh great is your works, and the thoughts are very deep, I thank you Lord. Even when the wicked spring forth, you cut them off like grass, so I don't have to fret the evil doers, you bring vengeance upon them. You said bless it the man that walk in your way. I thank you Lord that I desire to walk in your way. I purpose to walk in your way. I purpose to stay in your way; there-fore you will not cut me off, nor will you forsake my inheritance.

I thank you Lord, for being an ever presence help in the time of need. You my help, my soul would have fainted but you my help. My foot would have slipped but you my help. My thoughts would have ceased but you my help. Oh God you my defense, you the rock of my refuge. Oh God I come into your presence with thanksgiving, I make a joyful noise unto you with these psalms.

You are great, you are a great king. Your hands are on the deep place of the earth, the strength of the hills are also with you and you are providing for me your, your child. Praise you God! Harden not your heart against me, as in the day of provocation, don't let even my heart be harden toward you, but God avoid me from the temptation, that I might bow down in worship you. I just want to kneel down before you, for you are the Lord, my maker, the rainmaker. Oh God, give me a new song to sing unto you. I want to sing a new song unto you. I want to bless your name, give me a new song to sing.

As declare your glory among the heathens, I declare your wondrous before these people. Honor and majesty for you, strength and beauty is in your sanctuary. Oh Lord I give you glory, I give you glory due to your name. I bring you an offering. I come in your courts with an offering of praise, and I worship you God mighty everlasting one. Allow us to come back to worship in you God.

Let the heaven rejoice, and let the earth be glad, let the sea roar, and the fullness thereof let the field be joyful and all that is in, even the trees clap their hands in praise to you, the birds sing there song to praise you. We know you come to judge the earth, so keep our hearts and minds stayed on you. Oh Father, let your light so shine in us that others might see our good work and glorify you. Let your light be sold for righteousness and gladness, and the heart of the upright, that we might be glad in you. We want to give thanks at the remembrance of all you've done. We want to give thanks at the remembrance of your holiness. Fire goes before you, lighting goes before you and we acknowledge that all the mountains and the hills melting like wax before your mighty powers.

You are our God and we are your people. Please take us back to you once again dear Lord, and we will repent and truly glorify your name for your presence is what we long to have in our mist. Your voice and your sweet anointing we seek today. Help us Father, to be your own and value our salvation as a gift we will never give back. Today, on this altar of prayer, we praise you, we adore you and we leave a sacrifice of wanting more of you. In the mighty name of Jesus, be magnified in us today.

AMEN

Spiritual Warfare Prayer

Thou power of bad days, weeks, and months, die NOW, in the name of Jesus. Release yourself away from us. Be replaced with Gods goodness over our lives now, in the name of Jesus. Thou power of setback, die, in the name of Jesus. Any power flying to arrest my progress, fall down and die, in the name of Jesus. Power of reproach, die, in the name of Jesus. Any problem programmed to ridicule me, be expired. Agents of the grave summoned to appear in my dreams, die now. Vision killers, I stop you before you stop me. Anything burned to bury me, bury your owners.

O heavens, arise in thy might of perfection, perfect all that concerns me. O Lord, repair what should be repaired in my life. O God arise and disgrace every enemy against my increase. O God, arise, and speak words of creation into my situations. O God, arise, and cancel every consequence of any mistake made by me, in the name of Jesus. O God, arise, and let every enemy of my calling scatter, in the name of Jesus.

Jesus I separate myself from any evil tree representing my destiny, I curse the tree to die, in the name of Jesus. Sentences of the enemy upon my destiny, die, in the name of Jesus. Let the elements gather their resources to favor and promote my destiny. I establish the power of God upon you, oh earth, bless my destiny. You elements, you shall not hurt that which the Lord has blessed in my life. You shall not steal from my destiny. Thou power of evil handshakes, die, in the name of Jesus. Thou power of evil laying of hands, die now.

I use the keys of heaven to lock out problems from my life, in the name of Jesus. That which the devil has locked against me, angels open by fire. Anyone using dust and leaves against me, die now, in the name of Jesus. The powers of powders is wet and useless in my life now. Boomerang to the sender! Woe unto the powers bragging and boasting against my destiny, in the name of Jesus. Kidnapping power, I rebuke you by thunder, in the name of Jesus.

Every robber of destiny, assigned against my life, scatter, in the name of Jesus. Oh night, arise, gather strength against my enemies, in the name of Jesus.

Every intimidation of the wicked, break, in the name of Jesus. I wipe out the relevance of my enemies, in the name of Jesus. You shall not prevail over my God, the Almighty Jehovah. Yahweh reigns as my fighter and the lifter of my head, now, and throughout my generational DNA. My Father, let Your angels be provoked against my enemies, in the name of Jesus. By fire, by thunder, I war in the spirit of Elijah and Jehu, in the name of Jesus, I speak a "CYRUS" anointing on my life, NOW and forever more

In Jesus name

AMEN

Prayer for My Leaders and the World

Oh thou who trouble Apostle Dr. J G Rice, Bishop James Rice and (*your pastors name*), Greater Harvest Christian Center and (*your church name*) and all there partners, they will have to fight against the God of Elijah, and he shall trouble you TODAY. Every enemy of Apostle and Bishop Rice and (*your pastors name*) and all there partners shall scatter NOW, in Jesus name.

Oh God arise and up-root everything you did not plant inside Greater Harvest, Apostle and Bishop Rice, (*your pastor and church name*) and our members and partners. In the name of Jesus. I decree and declare that my church, my leaders and my personal family will experience the fire of REVIVAL in our lives and evangelism will be my bread, and the bread of our ministry. Let the fire of revival fall NOW upon my church, my pastor, and Greater Harvest Christian Center, Chief Apostle Dr. J G Rice and Bishop Rice, our members, our partners, family and friends.

God please let salvation continue to be in our walls and peace in our land. Let it the power of God fall now in our Lives, and the lives of our countrymen. Bless our President to have wisdom and avoid all snares and traps, for himself, his family and our country. Bless there to be world peace, beginning with America .

I pray the Glory of God over schools and prevent any harm and dangers to innocent children. I pray for war torn countries, that your Spirit of Salvation would move through the land, that none would be lost. I pray for food to be distributed to the needy, and that the greedy would not reign or prosper them to suffer because of their greed. Protect the animals that feed our bodies, from radical cancerous and diseased cells. Protect our water and sources of food, from terrors, by day and by night, protect our sources of living from contamination from the land skies, or under-ground.

Father we need you to give us the learned tongue so we will know what to pray for today. Help the elderly that have no one, calm their fears and remove the spirit of loneliness from them. Help those to be good parents whom you have granted the gift of life to, help those to be good children whom you have allowed others to breathe life within. Both spiritually and naturally. Provide for our needs according to your riches in Glory!

Let us become the blessed and the blessing. Let us become the head and not the tail, and let us experience the power of our Lord and Savior Jesus Christ. The yoke destroyer, the burden remover, the blessing restorer, the miracle working power of God. In Jesus name. Let it happen NOW!! My body, my soul, my mind, my spirit is in agreement, in Jesus name.

AMEN

I Am Chief Apostle, and This is a Time of Prayer

Let's pray…..I am praying for you

Heavenly Father, implant in our heart, we are doers of the Word according to your Word. We are in Jesus and Jesus is in us. We are the body of Christ, we are more than conquers through Christ; we are over comers and we overcome by the blood of Jesus and our testimonies. We love not our life unto death according to your Word; for we are the head and not the tail. We can do all things through Christ who strengthens us today, as we speak your Word we know that it will not return back to you void.

Your Word will accomplish what it was sent to do. If we ask anything, according to your will, God I know you'll hear us, and because you hear us we have whatsoever it is we are asking for. So Heavenly Father, we thank you for your word today. As it is written, we will not forget your benefits. You forgave all of our sins, you healed all of our diseases, and you have redeemed our lives from destruction. Lord, you have crowned us with loving-kindness and tender-mercies, you have satisfied our mouth with good things; our youth is renewed like an eagle. You are merciful, you are gracious, you are slow to anger, you are plenteous in your mercies and haven't dealt with us according to our iniquities.

As far as the heaven is high above the earth so great is your mercy towards us. So we fear you God, as far as the east is from the west. We have thrown our sin from us God. Now God gird our loins with your girdle of truth. You have set us free from bondage and strongholds. We operate in discernment and we continue to be free so we take off the dependency of the flesh, dependency of the law, and dependency of anything in this world. We trust and depend on you Jesus.

I thank you God that you are our healer; you are Jehovah Rophi, you are our provider; Jehovah Jireh. God I thank you that you have healed us and we declare that you are our help, our soundness in mind we have the healing of you God; by your stripes we are healed! We have a spiritual healing, a soul healing, a physical healing, healing in relationship; we've been redeemed from the curse of the law. We've been redeemed from sickness, we are redeemed from poverty, we are redeemed from spiritual death; we have the help from God.

We have the wealth of God, we have your soundness in spirit, your soundness in soul, and your soundness in body. We present our bodies as a living sacrifice Holy and acceptable unto you, which is our reasonable service. We are not conformed to this world, we are transformed by the renewing of our minds according to your to your Word. Lord you are on our side.

We fear no man, according to Word, we are over-comers from all strongholds and all bondages. We over-come by the blood of the lamb, we are cleansed from all unrighteousness. Oh God, the word is our testimony. Therefore the word we have hidden in our heart that we might not sin against you. We keep it in our hearts so we don't return to the strongholds. We don't love our life, but God we love you.

So we rebuke everything that doesn't line up with your word, and thank you God for all your blessings that will come upon us because we operate in the Spirit of Obedience. Your blessing will come upon us! We hear you God, and we thank you God. We can hear your voice and obey your voice. Thank you that our bodies are blessed, the fruit of our ground is blessed, our children our blessed, our possessions are blessed, our cattle is blessed, our business is blessed. The increase of our kind is blessed, our family is blessed, blessed our flock of our sheep; we have authority over these things. Blessed in the basket, oh Lord, blessed in the storehouse, our finances is blessed.

You have commanded a blessing on us oh Lord. Our storehouse is all set in your hands. You've blessed us in the land that you gave us and you have established us as a Holy people unto you. Oh God, you've promised to keep us, as we keep your commandments and walk in your way. Blessed are we God because we refuse to walk in the counsel of the ungodly. Nor will we stand in the way of the sinners, nor will we be seated in the seat of the scornful, for God we delight in your word and in your word do we meditate day and night.

We are like a tree, now planted by the rivers of living water, we bring forth fruit in season, and our leaves will not wither. Whatsoever everything, whatever anything, whatever everything we do shall prosper! God we bring all of our tithes into the storehouse that there is going to be sufficiency in your house, and you will prove us. Oh God, you will prove us, by opening up the windows of heaven and pouring us out a blessing. God you will prove us!

You are going to prove that we're faithful, and you are going to show the world that we're blessed. Oh God, we won't even have room to store it all; for as we have given freely, we will receive freely according to your Word. Your goodness and mercy shall follow us all the days of our lives, in you we will praise your Word, and we'll put our trust in you. We will fear no flesh; for what can flesh do to us? For the blood of Jesus is covering us, and we know all things work together for good because we love you, because we are called according to your purpose.

If you are for us, and God we know you are; no one can be against us. You are on our side according to your Word, now Lord we bring our request to you, Oh God; we bring our prayer list before you, we bring our personal concerns before you, we bring our families before you, we bring anything that is on our minds before you. We lay them at down at your feet now God, we cast down any imaginations, we cast down anything that exalts itself against the knowledge of God. Oh God, we know that you're the Prince of Peace; Oh God we worship you today, we honor you today, we thank you for peace sandals. We thank you God that you have given us peace to walk into.

We thank you God, that we walk in the spirit and we thank you God that we are killing this flesh daily, minute by minute, moment by moment, day by day, hour by hour, and week by week. We are crucifying our flesh God. We are determined to be lined up in your Word. We're determined to be better in your Word. We're determined to hear your Word. God put your Word in us. God we cover our feet with the preparation of the Gospel, we take off vanity, we take off pride, we take off darkness.

We come against ignorance and we thank you for being an ever present God, an everlasting hope, Jehovah Shemmah, Jehovah Rophi, and Jehovah Tsidkenu. We call on your name right now, we invoke your spirit, and we invoke your presence. We ask your for your Glory; let your Glory fill this house, Glorify us God Magnify us God, Exalt us God and let the light shine. Let others see our good works and glorify you.

You are the Father that's in heaven, let your spirit be upon us. You have anointed and appointed us to preach the good news; you have appointed us and anointed us to break yokes. You have sent us to bind up the broken hearted, to proclaim liberty to the captive, and to open up the prison to them that are bound. To tell them that this is the day of Jubilee, the acceptable year. Your day of vengeance to preach Zephaniah, to preach Obadiah, Zechariah and Jeremiah, to preach your Word.

To declare good things in your Word, to appoint them to mourn in

Zion! Oh my God, you have appointed us to cry out and spare not God and we worship you. As mighty trees, we are planted by the rivers of water and whatsoever we do shall prosper. Whatsoever we do shall bring forth fruit, whatsoever we do shall multiply! We are successful in you God as you order our steps in your word. We acknowledge your presence oh God, you are the Lord of the harvest. We worship you, you are the Lord of the Harvest! We lift up your name, you are the Lord of the Harvest! And we glorify you Father, our precious Lord! Father your precious, we glorify you! How precious you are God. Spirit of the Living God falls fresh in this place.

Spirit of the Living God bless our Bishop. Oh Lord we're calling on you, bless our Bishop with dreams, ideas and visions. With witty concepts that will bring blessings to the body of Christ. Oh God bless every member, one by one and name by name. Wrap them in your blood, wrap them in your love, wrap them in your principles, and wrap them in your glory. Yes Lord, yes. Oh God I intercede this morning as a gap stander. Take the devil out there way and off their ears, take him out their minds and off their backs. Put the devil under their feet, in the Name of Jesus! Oh God, I'm calling your name, there is nobody like you and no-one like you.

Oh God, you're the lily in the valley, you're the bright and morning star. God I glorify you! God you said if you'd be lifted up, so I cast my crown down and I lift you up Jesus. You said if you'd be lifted up, you will draw. God we need you to draw in this place, we need you to draw in our lives. We need to have fruit on the tree. God you said it, so I believe it!

God you said, "If my people who are called by my name will humble themselves, pray, and seek my face and turn from their wicked ways" you told us that you will heal our land. So God we're standing in the need of healing this morning. Heal the land, heal this dirt; heal it God! Line it up with your word, line it up.

Everything that's sick, imaginations, we cast them down. Lustful thoughts, we bind them up. We bind them up away from us, in the name of Jesus! Infirmities, every sickness, everything attacking our minds, attacking our blood, our foot and hands, bind up. We don't have arthritis, sickle cell or high blood pressure or sugar because you were wounded for our transgressions and bruised for our iniquities. The chastisement of your peace is upon us and by your stripes I am healed. I'm healed from the blood and no weapon formed against me is going to prosper!

In the name of Jesus

AMEN

I Decree I Have Favor

I believe in the Father Almighty, creator of heaven and earth. I believe in Jesus Christ, God's only Son, my Lord and savior. I believe He was conceived by the Holy Spirit. He was born of the Virgin Mary. He suffered under the Pontus Pilate. He was crucified dead and buried. I believe He aroused on the third day and He ascended into Heaven.

I believe He sits now at the right hand of the Father. I believe He will come to judge the living and the dead. I believe in the Holy Spirit. I believe in the church worldwide. I believe in the Communion of the Saints. I believe in the forgiveness of sins. I believe in the resurrection of the body and the life everlasting.

I decree I'm blessed. I decree I'm whole. I decree there's nothing missing in my life, nothing broken in my life. I decree that the blessing of the Lord make me rich in every area of my life and add no sorrow. I decree a bump a crump anointing for my fiancés, for my health, for my happiness, for my wellbeing, for my soul, for my spirit, and for my life. There is nothing dead in me except sin, he's dead in me, and he's dead to me, there-fore no portals are open for the enemy to abide.

I decree that every opening be filled with the glory of God, my nasal, my mouth, my ear, my cavities, my portals all magnetizes, and draw the spirit of the living God. There-fore being filled in him I decree I am the righteous of Christ Jesus. Wrong, wrong spirit, wrong motives, wrong thoughts, wrong actions, do not abide here. Righteousness abides, truth abides, love abides, joy abides, peace abides I'm filled with the fruits of spirits. I'm filled with temperance, I add to my faith, I have virtue, I have integrity, I have character that pleases God. There-fore my angels are always on assignment to bring me the best for less, red dot special.

I decree people give me things, people work with me, I have a workable spirit, and they want to bless me, because of the God in me. I decree and declare I am faithful to God. I am faithful to the ministry. I am faithful in my giving; I am faithful in my worship. "Hallelujah" The favor of the Lord is mine. When I woke up this morning, his mercy was new on my life. I receive new mercy. Yesterday is covered and gone. Anything that's not like God is crop failure. I pour the spiritual gasoline on it, and I light it up to be burned away with the fire of the Holy Ghost. Only that which remains will be the purity.

I decree it shall follow me from day to day. Goodness and mercy shall bring it with them, as they follow me. Land and wealth are donated to me to enhance my life and Kingdom Assignment. I decree I will dwell in the house of the Lord, and that what I will seek after. I decree I will enhance and advance the kingdom of God, and that will I seek after. I decree that the word is mouth piece, and that will I seek after. I decree my prayer life is my strength for I find joy in prayer, and that will I seek after.

I use this decree to cover like-minded saint's other's in the body of Christ, that have this same desire, and I unite my faith with their faith. I become an intercessor, and I decree and the atmosphere for their life's, for their children life's, for there ministries life's. I decree I'm a person, a woman, or man of faith, and excellent. I decree I'm God's anointing. I decree he's working on my behalf. I decree when I go to bed and rise up there's a blessing at my door., my footsteps demand blessings to my life. I open my door at expectation to be blessed by the Lamb of God..

In the mighty name of Jesus

AMEN

We Decree We Will Come Back To God Prayer

Oh God we glorify your name. We bow down before you God, we ask that you here us being needed for your spirit right now. Be merciful to us Lord, for we cry unto you daily. Oh God rejoice in the soul of your servant, for unto thee Lord Do I lift up my soul, for thou Oh Lord are good and ready to forgive. You are plenteous and mercy to all those that call unto you. Give ear oh God to our prayers, Lord attend to the voice of our supplication.

Lord we call on you "Now" so in the day of trouble when we call unto you, you will answer us. Lord among all the little God's, we realize there's none like you God. Neither are there any works like your works, for all nations whom you have made shall come and worship you. Oh Lord, Hallelujah Jesus, Hallelujah Jesus. We come and worship you, for you are great, and you do wondrous things. We ask you to teach us your way that we may walk in your truth. Unite our hearts to fear your name "Oh God"

We will praise you, Oh our God with all our hearts; we will glorify your name. Lord we glorify your name forever more, for great are your mercy toward us, you delivered our soul from the lowest of hell. Oh God the pride might even try to rise up against us, and even the assembly of the violent people may seek after us, but God you will not set us before them, for you are full of compassion, you are gracious, long-suffering, patience, and truth. So turn unto us oh God and have mercy unto us, give us strength.

Lord give strength to your servants, save your handmaiden, In the name of Jesus. Save your male children, In the name of Jesus. Show us a token for good, that those that hate us may see us rise and the presence of you God that they will not be ashamed and we will not be ashamed, because you have help us God, you have comfort us, "Oh God." You are the foundation of our sanctification. You are the foundation of our destination. You are the right and ready just God. Oh God you are the hope of our hope. Set us free even in the pits of our mind, you set us free even in the pits of our emotions.

You have called us to the altar for this time of prayer. Oh God we low ourselves before you. Oh God we debased ourselves that you may exalt us. Glorious is your name, oh God in the mighty name of Jesus. Oh God we call on Mount Zion night and day, that you might be able to console us, even in the midst of our entire situation. We thank you God because you have established us, in the name of Jesus.

We call forth the singers and the worshippers right now. Oh God that we might sing a new song to the God of our salvation, in the name of Jesus. Oh Lord all night and all day we cry before thee. Our prayers come before you God; we ask that you hear our cry. Oh God you free us from among the dead, in the name of Jesus. You free us from lying spirits. You free us from doubt and unbelief. You free us from those things that are hopeless, every grave clothes we ask that you shake it off "Now" in the mighty name of Jesus. Oh God we don't have another help other than you God. From the north and south we cry unto you, we are broken father, but yet we are whole because of your blood. So we ask you God our lover and our friend to be a gate around us, to compass all around us, to keep our soul from affliction, in the might name of Jesus. Wondrous works be known unto us. Show your loving kindness God. Show your faithfulness. Show your wondrous works towards us, in the mighty name of Jesus.

We ask you now God, even as we ask you to come into our hearts, come into our mind, encompassed us to the more God. For you are great, and greatly to be praised. You are great, and greatly to be feared. You are great, and greatly and the Assembly of God to be reverence. And God we reverence your holy name, for your seed you have established forever. You build up a throne and all generation. You made a covenant with us, even as you have done with our father Abraham, and our father David, and our father Isaac, and our father Jacob. Oh God you a covenant keeper and the midst of it all God.

You a covenant keeper, you a mind regulator, we give your name praise, you beat down our foes before our face, and you send plague to take them away from us. You run our foes to the river and there they loose, because you allow that same river to encompass them, that you don't allow them to encompass us. Oh God, in the might name of Jesus. We thank you for your glory, for you have made your glory to come all around us. We thank you God, you broke down all the hedges, and all the strong holds. You make void the covenant of the un-faithful, but with us God you established a covenant forever.

We thank you God for the first fruit, bringing you the first praise, giving you the first born, giving you the first offering, giving the first of everything. We wake up, we acknowledge you in all our ways and you direct our paths. You've been our dwelling path in all generation, before the mountains where brought forth, before you formed the earth, and the world, from everlasting to everlasting you are God. We thank you God that trouble don't last always. In the morning the joy comes. In the morning the faithfulness of your word return unto us in the morning.

We thank you Lord, for we know the power of you. So teach us to number our days, that we may apply our hearts to wisdom. Satisfy us early with your mercy that we may rejoice all our days. Thank you now for the angels that you give charge over us. Thank you now God, we abide under the shadow of the almighty, as we dwell in the secret place of the most high. We will say of you that you are our fortress, you are our refuge. We can say that we trust in you God. We can say that you delivered us from the fowler, from the noisome pestilence, that you cover us with your feathers, you cover us under your wings, and we trust in you.

You are our shield; you are our buckler, in the name of Jesus. We trust in you God, there's no evil that cometh our way, no evil shall befall us, no plague shall come nigh our dwelling. You have given these angels charge over us, to keep us we will not dash our hand or foot against a stone.

We will trample upon the lion. We will trample upon the dragon, and we will trample them under our feet, in the mighty name of Jesus. Because you set your love on us, there-fore God you deliver us, because you set us on high. I thank you Lord you said we can call on your name in you will answer us. You said you satisfy us with long life, thank you Lord for long life, thank you Lord for long prosperous life. Thank you Lord we give thanks unto you, it's a good thing to give thanks unto you Lord. Yes lord we sing praises unto your name for you've shown forth your loving kindness, even in the morning you've been faithful to us God, even in the night, so we give your name praise.

With our hands we clap them and make glad, even with our voice we lift it up and say thank you. We lift our voice like a unicorn horn and you anoint us with fresh oil. We give you glory, we shall see our desires come to pass in our life. Yes Lord we shall flourish, because we are planted in the courts of God. Thank you Lord we still bring forth fruit in old age. We will be fat and will flourish. We will be faithful, available, and teachable, and will flourish, and we will show that the Lord is upright. He is my rock; there is no unrighteousness in you Lord.

You made me glad; I triumph in your works. You made me glad; I triumph in the works of your hands. Oh great is your works, and the thoughts are very deep, I thank you Lord. Even when the wicked spring forth, you cut them off like grass, so I don't have to fret the evil doers, you bring vengeance upon them. You said bless it the man that walk in your way. I thank you Lord that I desire to walk in your way. I purpose to walk in your way. I purpose to stay in your way; there-fore you will not cut me off, nor will you forsake my inheritance. I thank you Lord, for being an ever presence help in the time of need.

You're my help, my soul would have fainted but you my help. My foot would have slipped but you my help. My thoughts would have ceased but you my help. Oh God you my defense, you the rock of my refuge. Oh God I come into your presence with thanksgiving, I make a joyful noise unto you with these psalms. You are great, you are a great king. Your hands are on the deep place of the earth, the strength of the hills are also with you. Harden not your heart against me, as in the day of provocation, don't let even my heart be harden toward you, but God avoid me from the temptation, that I might bow down in worship you.

I just want to kneel down before you, for you are the Lord my maker. Oh God give me a new song to sing unto you, I want to sing a new song unto you. I want to bless your name, give me a new song to sing. As declare your glory among the heathens, I declare your wondrous before these people. Honor and majesty for you, strength and beauty is in your sanctuary. Oh Lord I give you glory, I give you glory due to your name. I bring you an offering. I come in your courts with an offering of praise, and I worship you God mighty everlasting one.

Let the heaven rejoice, and let the earth be glad, let the sea roar, and the fullness thereof, let the field be joyful and all that is in, even the trees clap their hands in praise you, the birds sing there song to praise you.

We know you come to judge the earth, so keep our hearts and minds stayed on you. Oh father let your light so shine in us that others might see our good work and glorify you. Let your light be sold for righteousness and gladness, and the heart of the upright, that we might be glad in you. We want to give thanks at the remembrance of all you've done. We want to give thanks at the remembrance of your holiness.

Amen

Prayer of Thanksgiving

Thank you God! We praise you Lord. We thank you Lord, We thank you Jesus, everlasting Father, Prince of Peace. We come alive in worship, God we adore you.

We thank you Lord in the Name of Jesus. Yushewa we give you praise. Yahweh we give you praise. We glorify your mighty name God. In you we live and move and have our being God. We will decree your goodness God. We will decree your mercy. We will decree your grace. We will decree your purpose in our lives.

We set our face like a flint to give your name Praise. We will come alive in our Spirit We will come alive in our Faith. We will take it to another Level; In the Name of Jesus. In your Name God, a sweet hour of prayer that call me from a world of care and bids me at my Father's Throne!

Make all my wishes and wants known in season of distress, and grief. My soul has found relief! And often escape the tempters snare, now Lord we come to you in Prayer. "Yes God," stir me up again. Put the Fire of Grace on me that we remain thankful. Put the Fire of the Holy Ghost on me, in the Name of Jesus. That will allow me every day to see your grace, power, and love for me.

I am grateful and thankful today for my salvation, health, many blessings, family, friends, church, and my financial independence and abundance of prosperity. Father thank you for precious life and joy in my life. Smiles and hugs and a right sound mind to love and know you. Thank you for all gifts of the body, mind, and spiritual functions.

AMEN

AMEN

AMEN

Set Us Free and Give Us the Bondage Releasing Anointing

But we need a breakthrough, just like you did for Paul and Silas at midnight. You shook the prison doors. We are calling on your Name, open up our bondages and set us free.

Open up our mindset and set us free

Open up our doubt and unbelief and set us free.

Open up our money and set us free

Open up our relationship and set us free

"SET US FREE"

Set us free from drugs

Set us free from alcohol

Set us free from cigarettes

Set us free from lying

Set us free from being un-wise in our money

Set us free from being dumb minded

Set us free from being stupid

Set us free from being ignorant

We need a set free moment

Yes God, at midnight, I need you to shake my corridors, shake my walls

Shake the things that hold me back and set me free, In the Name of Jesus

I got to be free; you came that I might be free

I want to be free, kill the old man, and kill the flesh

"KILL IT GOD!" Crucify it, jack it, slap it, strip it; that I might have more of you God.

AMEN

Prayer of Evangelism

We cry out for our loved ones that you will save, that you will heal, that you redirect; in the Name of Jesus. So many falling by the wayside.

So many don't know who you are, but God send your saving Spirit. Send your saving Spirit in this land, this country; one more time!

Send your saving Spirit throughout this nation, time and time again! Send your saving Spirit; save from the North, South, East, and West.

Save God, deliver our family members. Oh God, strengthen the hand of your salvation once again.

We have children that need to be saved. We have family members that need to be saved. Lord we don't have time to sleep.

We come to call their name out before you. Save Mother's, save brothers, sisters, uncles, nieces, nephews, cousins, and neighbors. Oh God, save them!

Send down your rain of Fire. Let them know the wages sin is death, but the gift of God is still eternal life. We need that Eternal Life, and Light; now in the name of Jesus.

Send eternal life, send eternal fire oh God. We're calling out for souls right Now! Yes Lord, there still standing ion the need of prayer.

Somebody ask me to pray today, God if I've forgotten, stir it up in me that I might retrieve to the Throne Room of Grace for them right now.

Somebody is depending on me. Somebody is depending on me to

call their name. Everybody that sow seed in this ministry, continue to save them. Continue to keep them healed. Continue to keep them stirred up.

Yes God, they're planting their finances, but in return give them a Miracle. Give them a breakthrough right now, in the Name of Jesus. Got to have a breakthrough in the Name of Jesus. You know our struggle, you know our pain, and you know our difficulties!

In Jesus name

AMEN

Oh God, Save Them Prayer

My soul has found relief and often express the tempest care. I come to you God, yes God, stir me up again. Put the fire of grace on me. Put the fire of the Holy Ghost on me in the name of Jesus. We cry out for our love ones. That you will save, that you will heal, that you direct in the name of Jesus. Oh God, I want to cry out for the lost, I want to cry out for the lost souls. In the name of Jesus. So many are falling by the waste side. So many don't know who you are, but God send your saving spirit. Send your sowing spirit into this land, country, one more time

Send your Saving Spirit throughout this nation Lord. Save from the north, south, east and west. Save God! Deliver our family members. Oh God, strengthen the hand of your salvation once again. We have children that need to be saved. We have family members that need to be saved. Lord we don't have time to sleep.

We came to call out the name of _____ before you. Save mothers, fathers, brothers, sisters, save uncles, nieces, nephews, cousins, and the neighbors. Oh God save them. Send down your rain of fire, of salvation. Let them know the wages of sin is death, but the gift of God is still eternal life.

We need that eternal life right now, in the name of Jesus, to visit our family, friends, neighbors and co-workers. Even our enemies, those who despitefully use us, we need your spirit to fall on us, now, phenomenally and powerfully. Send eternal life, send eternal fire. Oh God, we're calling out for souls right now. You didn't save us to lay in defeat, but you saved us to make a midnight cry. Yes Lord, their standing in a need of prayer.

Stir it up in me that I might entreat the throne room of grace for them right now. Somebody is depending on me to lift their name for salvation. Somebody is depending on me to call their name, I call the name of _____. I pray now for the 120 partners, covenant partners, members, members families, our co-laborers of the Gospel and their ministries. Everybody that sow seeds in this ministry, continue to save them. Your fivefold leaders, we lift up to you, now. Continue to keep them healed. Continue to keep them stirred up to all who support us financially. Bless them and save their loved ones.

Yes God, they're planting their finances, but in their return give them a miracle. Give them a break through, right now, in the name of Jesus. God we need a breakthrough, in the name of Jesus. We must have a breakthrough cry, in the name of Jesus. You know our struggles, you know our pain, and you know our difficulties. But we need a break through, just like you did for Paul and Silis at midnight. You shook the prison doors, we're calling on your name.

Open up our bondages and set us free, open up our mind-set and set us free. Open up our doubt and unbelief and set us free. Take us to another level in you set us free. Open up our money and set up free. Open up our relationships and set us free. Set us free! Set us free from drugs and alcohol. Set us free from cigarettes. Set us free from lying. Set us free from being unwise with our money. Set us free from being dumb, set us free being stupid. Set us free from being ignorant. We need a set free movement.

Yes God, at midnight, we need you to shake, shake, shake, many more doors. Now! Shake our halls, shake our walls, shake the things that us back and set us free, in the name of Jesus. We have to be free! You came so that we might be free.

We want to be free! Kill the old man, kill the flesh. Kill it! God, crucify it! Jack it! Slap it! Strip it! So that we might have more of you God.

In Jesus name

AMEN

Prayer for Those In Need of Salvation

Please God of our salvation, save our children, save our uncles, save our aunts, save our sisters, save our brothers, save our mothers, save our fathers. Yes God, don't let my family go to hell, while I'm shouting going to heaven. I call out there names before you in the name of Jesus. I lift up these souls _____. God I know the power that is already in this house. While they are asleep you're shaking their beds, in the name of Jesus. The precious lamb, he still saving. I believe you are still saving. Give our family a miracle. Save them, from the elder to the youngest, in Jesus name. Save now God, by the power of prayer.

The precious lamb, the blood it's still working. I send the blood of Jesus after _____. I send the Holy Ghost hound dog after them. I send the Holy Ghost Hound-dog to snatch them out of sin. Save every complacent spirit, in the name of Jesus. Shake it up! Save my co-workers in the name of Jesus. Put the fire of the Holy Ghost in their life, that we might do kingdom work together. God I need salvation to visit my house. I'm like Nicodemus, I'm coming to you at night. Nicodemus said, Lord what must I do to be save. You have to be born of the water and the spirit. God some of us are born of the water, but not of the Spirit. Save our family members, I intercede on their behalf. I stand in the gap for them. You saved me God so that I could call someone else into the kingdom.

Move in compassion and save them. God I come to meet you for business. Save our family members, in the name of Jesus. Fill them with the Holy Ghost. I come to make war. I come for victory. Yes, Lord I know you can do it because you did it for me. You took me out of sorrow, you took me out of shame. You put my foot on a rock to stay and you are still saving. I strip the Lesbian Spirit. I expose the Homosexual Spirit and I say turn your life over to God.

I expose the whore-monger. I expose the back-biter. I expose the doubter and unbeliever, and I say get right with God. And do it now! Get right with God. Get right with God and he will show you how. Get right with God and let the blood move.

I come against every religion spirit and say get right with God. I come against every spirit, every ugly thing that will exalt it's self against the will of God. I say the blood, the blood, Satan the blood is against you. You will not pervert our nation, the bible say's when two and three will come together that He will be in the midst of us. I know God is here, I believe Him, I ask Him. He said ask what you will and it shall be given unto you. In the name of Jesus, I want to see _____ saved. I want to see families giving their hearts to God. See families getting delivered, turning down drugs, turning around the drug man. See them living Holy and see them being righteous. See them coming up to another level. See them pulling somebody else up. See them telling others to be saved. See them stretching out.

I call forth my family members back into the Kingdom. Your talent shall not be lost. You shall come forth as pure gold, in the name of Jesus.

God I believe you heal mind sets. God is able to set them free even in their minds and in their actions. God you can do anything, but fail. God put me in my family so I can call out the name of those that need to be saved. That it will be in the atmosphere, that the devil can loose the influence that's in their life. The spirit of the living God will begin to twirl in their way. Those children of yours that is living un-Godly life-styles we come against it, in the name of Jesus. We come against any haughtiness, fake-hood, in the name of Jesus. We know they're not walking right towards God. We will decree and snatch them by the power of the Holy Ghost.

We will break free, break them FREE GOD! Break every chain, oh

God. I don't know how you're going to do it, but I believe you will and I know you can. Break Free! Break Free! Break free their minds, break their emotions from being caught up with the devil. Break free from the argumentative spirit. They try to reject the word, I break them free from their stupidity. I break them free from their mind set. They will respect the word of God. I have the key to open up my family. I have the key to open up salvation inside of _____. I have a key to open up salvation in my DNA and I'm going to use the key to the kingdom. I decree I'm going to work my salvation. I'm going to work like a mother in Zion. I'm going to birth and bring forth. Nothing is not going to be given to me, I'll have to push it out. The crisis is now! My family needs you now! It's a midnight cry and it's a break-through cry. It's a deliverance cry and a get save cry. I'm tired of my family members dying from dope, dying with no hope, and playing church. Oh God, move through our families.

Yes God, do something. We're believers in you! We repent for not crying out to you. We repent for not being serious. But, oh God, you're able to take our family members a mind that is distorted by drugs. Yes, our family maybe in sin; but save them. I don't want to close my compassion. I don't want to close my bowels, because if it had not been for you God I wouldn't be here. Oh God, so move Jesus. If you haven't chose me, that would have been me and I would have needed somebody to pray for me right now. God, I ask according to your tender mercies, that you will move like you move over the earth and cover my family so that they will be saved. One by one, name by name, I call down the strong holds on our families, rather it be the grandmother, grandfather, uncles or aunts. I call in the ancestors and tell you that you have no root over us. In the name of Jesus!

I expose you and come against the source, the root of it all and tell you, you can't live in our house. You can't live, you must die, that we may live, in the name of Jesus! Root it up! Pull it out, send salvation to cover it all. Whether it's molestation, homosexuality; whether it's anger, bitterness or strife. Root it up! Whether it's family separation and division, root it up, in the name of Jesus. Whether it's greed of selfishness, root it up God. Pull it up out of our families so they might be saved, in the name of Jesus. Strong man we bind you! Whether it's liquor, wine, partying, sex, money or whatever it is, we bind it up! The word says, unless we bind the strong man he has root over the house. So we bind that demon strong man off our family that will keep them from being saved.

We bind up the Spirit of Jealousy. Jealousy over them that are saved. When the family is talking to other family members about the one who's saved, that spirit tries to turn the family against them. Jealousy, evil demon! We cast you away from our families, that they might see the light from darkness.

We bind up the Spirit of Compromise. When people don't won't to tell other's when their wrong, we cancel this assignment. Our families will be saved. We call it out of our family's roots demon and expose you. We expose it so that our family can be saved. We call it down! We expose the things that made us captive, so we can set our family's free. We expose it now! Today salvation will enter into our family's houses. We bind the Spirit of Perversion. We expose it today, that my family might be saved. That the hurt can be heal in the name of Jesus.

We bind up the Spirit of Self Pride. We tear down the strongman, so that the Spirit of Salvation can come into our family. Every evil root, fruit, and tentacle we tear it down tonight, so that the spirit of salvation can come in. We tear it down, it will not affect another generation. We decree it today and we will see instant results. They're going to get better not worse. They're going to come closer not further, in the name of Jesus. They don't have to know that we prayed for them, but we're going to see results and our families are going to see it. We're going to know that the hand of

God is on our families.

We give God glory.

We shout for our families by putting praise on every name spoke of.

In Jesus name.

AMEN

Chief Apostle Dr. J. G. Rice

Rebuking the Curse Off Our Families Finances

Lord, touch my family to begin to pay their tithes and offerings, so our family will not be cursed. Mold and shape them until they yield to the power of tithes and offerings. Until they can't wait to give that 10, 15, 20 percent; that you might take the curse off their lives Lord. You said, in your word that if we don't tithe lord you will curse us with a curse. God you have not removed that!

So let your people be obedient that we will see more, have more, do more and gain more because of the obedience of your word. I come against every excuse against being obedient to you word and your commandments. Lord as your word has spoken it, and we see it, let us receive your word like hungry children. We will pay our tithes and offerings.

In the name of Jesus, Lord let us tell our families to pay their tithes and offerings so that the curse can come of their lives. Lord let us know that it's not about one person getting money, but it's about being obedient to your commandments. Train our minds that we might not sin against you. Train our hearts that we won't go into direct disobedience, in the name of Jesus.

Lord thank you for the blessings that are on this camp; this tribe of Judah! Thank you, as you are the lion of the tribe of Judah. God, thank you. As we are obedient we will eat the fat of the land. Thank you for keeping us in obedience to your word. Teach us how to number our days, how to move in set time and divine destiny. Teach us how to move in kingdom dominion and promises and principles.

God, I thank you now and I give your name praise and we receive it is done God; we receive it as done. We just want to believe and receive. Make us mustard trees that we just believe and receive. Grow us out of mustard seeds faith and into mustard tree faith.

God we want to be mustard trees. You said as a mustard tree, that the fowls of the air would come enlarge in our branches. Lord, mature us and grow us up so that we'll be a mustard tree church. Financial wealth and perpetual wealth, shall abide in my family as we obey. Oh God, let the seed finally go into the ground and bring forth good fruit. I honor you, I praise you, and I worship you. I worship you! I worship you!

Thank you Jesus, you've been waiting oh so very long but the struggle is over now. God, we receive your peace. Hallelujah, Thank you Jesus. Thank you God, we praise you Lord, we thank you Lord, We thank you Jesus. Everlasting Father. Prince of peace, we come alive in worship. God we adore you. We thank you Lord, in the name of Jesus. Yeshua, we give you praise. We glorify your mighty name God. In you we live and move and have our being God.

We will decree your mercy on our finances.

We will decree your grace on our finances.

We will decree your purpose in our lives and on our finances.

We set our face like a flint to give your name praise for our finances.

We will come alive in our spirit and our finances.

We will come alive in our faith, our money will populate, repopulate, and GROW!

We will take it to another level in the name of Jesus.

In your name God, you will do great triumph in us. Our family shall make an impact of social contributions because of Kingdom wealth.

In your name God, sweet hour of prayer that called me from a world of care, and bids me at my father throne. Make all my wishes and wants know in season or distress and grievance.

My soul has found relief and often express the tempest care. I come to you God, yes God, stir me up again. Put the fire of grace on me. Put the fire of the Holy Ghost on me in the name of Jesus. We cry out for our love ones. That you will save, that you will heal, that you direct in the name of Jesus. Oh God, I want to cry out for the lost, I want to cry out for the lost souls. In the name of Jesus. So many are falling by the waste side. So many don't know who you are, but God send your saving spirit. Send your sowing spirit into this land, country, one more time.

      Jesus.

      Amen

Prayer of Repentance

We thank you tonight God and we glorify your name for life, and health, and well-being. Father hallow be your name. We praise you for your kingdom, that is to coming and for your will to be on earth, as it is in Heaven. God we ask you that you will give us this day our daily bread, forgive us of all our debts, forgive us for all our transgression, and forgive us for all our iniquities. Holy Spirit blot out everything God that will put up a sign against us, in the name of Jesus. Hide it behind your blood, in the name of Jesus. We know God that we are reformed from all of our sins, and we accepted you as our Lord and Savior. Heavenly Father we ask that you have mercy on us tonight.

Please forgive us God, please have mercy and grace our God, in the name of Jesus. We know you took our place on Calvary, and our debts are paid through your blood, sweet Jesus, son of the living God, we beg for forgiveness tonight for all sins known and unknown. We humbly ask you God, that you will wash away all of our sin, iniquities, all of our transgression, all of our slackness, all of our doubt, all our unbelief, Lord please limit the place where the enemy has reign in us. So we ask you to fill us from the crown of our heads to the soles of our feet and back from the soles of our feet to the crown of our head.

The blood of Jesus, we need you tonight, like music in the atmosphere. God we need you ,we cant do anything without you, our God. Oh Jesus, we don't need to have any words, but that you will know it is the music of our heart. Jesus play a song in us tonight, we want to be your symphony of praise, that you might be glorified. Receive our songs, prayers, and worship, in Jesus name. Set our hearts for this is our time with you.

We rebuke every Pharisee in our lives. We rebuke every republican in our lives. And we thank you God that when we come into your presence, we don't come like the Pharisees, nor like the republicans, but God we ask you to be gracious unto us, and have mercy unto us. We thank you God that there's no tragedies that befalling in our lives right now. We thank you that there's no mishaps, and no misunderstanding, no any illegal judgments that's coming up against us God. For the Holy Spirit has covered us therefore were not bitter, were not resentful, we are not moving in un-forgiveness we want set our pattern of thinking like those that have no hope, We recognize that all things work together for the good of those for us that love you.

We love you God. Lord if we have lost our "Spiritual Equilibrium," we ask you to get us back into balance. If we come with a Spirit of Polerism, not obeying the direct word of our covenant... if we worship idol gods... if we worship modern culturalism...If we worship religion idols, oh God, we want to repent tonight. For you said in your word, if your people will turn away from sin you would heal our land! Oh God, we ask you now, rather it be individual or collectively, to move God, in the midst of your people on our behalf. Move God Elohim, justify your blood, for we believe God that you took away all of our sin, and the sin of mankind that we can be righteous before you. Lord Jesus, that you raised from the dead, just so we can be righteous before you.

Tonight God fill us with your Holy Spirit. Even though we might have a measure of your Spirit, God fill us with your Holy Spirit even more! We ask for your wisdom, the wisdom that comes from the true living God. The wisdom, that comes from the word of God. The wisdom, that comes from the peace of God. The wisdom, that comes from the boldness of God. We want you to breathe on us Jesus. Breathe on us with the Holy Ghost power. Breathe on us with humbleness. Breathe on us with faithfulness come in the room Jesus, like a mighty rushing wind, like you did in the day of Pentecost fill us up "Oh God" until it runs over Jesus.

Thank you Lord for baptizing us, not just with water, but with fire of the Holy Ghost. Thank you Lord for baptizing us, not just with tongue, but with interpretation and utterances. Thank you Lord for baptizing us, not just with a heart to serve you, but with a heart to stay delivered. Thank you Lord for baptizing us not just to save us, but giving us the mindset and wanting somebody else to be saved, as your Ministry of Fire in evangelism. Thank you Lord for baptizing us in the anointing of fire and healing us, our God, in miracles, signs, and wonders.

We pray now God that your wisdom falls on us in the hidden part of our lives. Make us to know your wisdom according to your word. Teach us to number our days, so we will walk right before you. Teach us to be happy in you, for happiness is better than fine Gold. Teach us "Oh God" to have knowledge of you that you establish the Heaven in the Earth that you made these dust suits that we call a body and that you anoint from the crown of our head to the soul of our feet. Let our eyes have understanding of your will; let our ears hear from the throne room of grace. Let our lips utter your praise. "Yes Lord" we thank you now for sending Jesus, who respects your power when in this earth.

We thank you now that He has the ability to save our souls and redeem us to you! We thank you that He had the ability to raise up from the dead, and now He sitting by your right hand God making intersession for us. So we know who Jesus is, we thank you for the Holy Ghost. We want to pray with all your righteousness and a pure mindset for Israel and for Jerusalem. Lord we pray for Israel according to the book of Romans, oh God you say bless those that bless Jerusalem, so we bless Jerusalem. We give you honor and praise among all the people on the earth. We thank you that you are going to restore Israel. We thank you that you are going to restore Jerusalem. We thank you God.

We pray now God for America. We pray now for our President,

bless our President _____ , bless him/her and his/her family, bless the words in deeds, and his hands. Lord you said the word and hands of Kings and Priests there in your hands. So God do with them what you will have them to do, bless every servant of their house to be loyal, faithful, and true to their leadership and to the safety of our nation, in the mighty name of Jesus.

Bless the advisor and the assistant to the President, bless their spouse and their children let it be peace in there house that they can serve you without iniquities, so they can serve you without condemnation. Bless the Governors of this Land. Bless the Mayors. Bless the cities, providences, states, capitals and all lots and lands. Lord whisper in their ears while they sleep at night, be that Angel that will come in on the winds from God to grant them perfect directions. Be that voice that will speak to them concerning what's wrong. Do not allow the law makers to violate your biblical will or directions. Lord you know how to send an Angel to shake the very bed they sleep on make it well for your saints God. Do not allow us to suffer because of violent, evil or ungodly laws.

Make it be right for your saints God, make it to be right for the people that love you. Make it to be right for the people who adore you. Make it to be right for the people that are under your blood. Let me not be ashamed, let not my enemies triumph over me. Oh God of my Salvation, we come to you now in the name of Jesus. And we thank you God, we decree and declare things that's going to be good for us that they are going to be establish for us, that this is the year of our establishment. That this is the year of our breakthrough! This is the year of our promise! This is the year that you have mercy on us while mercy can be found. Oh God, assure us in the depths of our heart, as we keep your commandments and as we abide in you. As we abide in your love. As we live in your word. As we trust in your commandments. As we trust in your word. As we delight to do things that's concerning you God.

We thank you God for your word. We thank you for your truth.

We thank you for your righteousness. We thank you we are born of you, and we don't habitually practice sin. For your nature abides in us, and we cannot practice the work of the flesh, because we are born of you God. Move in our faith right now God. Build our faith right now God do surgery God.

We do not call wrong right, or right wrong. Let us be impartial in our discernment of your word. Give us today faith, peace, joy and love. Make me a friend to attract friends. Provide peace in these things concerning us, in Jesus name. We receive all your blessing of grace and peace concerning us NOW, in Jesus name

AMEN

Chief Apostle Dr. J. G. Rice

Breaking the Back of the Enemy

Any power pressing my head down, I shake you into the fire of God
In the name of Jesus.

I speak to my mind to TRANSFORM into the newness of CHRIST. Satanic agents assigned to stop me, I stop you before you stop me,
In the name of Jesus.

Satanic coma or full stop assigned to detain me, vanish,
In the name of Jesus.

Opportunity aborters, I puncture your powers,
In the name of Jesus.

Every altar of satanic delay, catch fire,
In the name of Jesus.

My hidden treasures buried in secret, come forth now,
In the name of Jesus.

Yokes assigned to frustrate my efforts, break,
In the name of Jesus.

Where is the Lord God of Elijah? Move me forward by fire,
In the name of Jesus.

Oil of favor from heaven, baptize my head,
In the name of Jesus.

Evil fingers pointed against my destiny, wither,
In the name of Jesus.

Any invisible chain on my legs, break, by the blood of Jesus and in the mighty name of the conquering KING!

In the name of Jesus.

Anointing for victory laughter, fall upon my life,

In the name of Jesus.

Barriers and strongholds erected to stop me, scatter,

In the name of Jesus.

Anti-progress enchantments and divination, backfire,

In the name of Jesus.

Every power adding sluggishness to my breakthroughs, die,

In the name of Jesus.

My mouth, receive the anointing of the over comer,

In the name of Jesus.

Thou Great Physician, heal my root, NOW!

In the powerful name of the undefeated one, Jesus Christ.

Ancient gates blocking my laughter, catch fire,

In the name of Jesus.

My Father, enlarge my coast to a dumbfounding degree,

In the name of Jesus.

My Father, my Father, pull darkness away from my environment,

In the name of Jesus.

Evil loads on my father's house, die,

In the name of Jesus.

Father, give me a glory that cannot be doubted.

In the name of Jesus.

Amen

NOTES

Prayer for The Author

I lift up my leader(s) *(leader's name)*. I ask you father to please create a special and powerful blessing for my leader and the shepherd of my soul. My pastor is a leader after your own heart towards the sheep here that they lead. Jehovah Nissi, I pray for them as they have prayed for me. I cover them with success and open door opportunity as they cover me daily. Protect all that concerns them and their families, Keep their bodies healed and their spiritual needs met as they meet our needs.

Father of health, breath health upon their heads today and provide and super natural blessing like never before. I also ask you Jehovah Jireh, please bless the author of this book, their staff, and family. That they would have no backlash for exposing us to Kingdom prayers and helping us to increase our time at the altar with you. Chief-Apostle Dr. J G Rice, Arch Bishop James Rice, all the saints of Greater Harvest Christian Center Churches Worldwide, and the InterGlobal Association of Christian Churches Worldwide, are covered now in the blood of Jesus. I decree and command and order this book to come into millions of hands of prayer warriors, intercessors, gap standers, and prayer leaders, for the cause of a deeper relationship with God our Father, the Great I am.

Lord Jesus, the keeper of our soul, and Holy Spirit our comforter, we acknowledge that Chief Apostle Dr. J G Rice is our Kingdom Ambassador, and a Master Prophet of God's word. I do decree as well, a financial blessing over their lives and that this book will be funded to reach the world, by the power of Jesus our Savior and King. We place them now under the fortress and the shadow of your wings and your love and your protection. The blood of Jesus is over this author and this work. May our hearts be turned to prayer for the leaders that guide us, individually, spiritually and corporately and bless them as they direct us in our spiritual growth.

I pray for the church body universally and corporally. I also ask your provisions for my brothers, sisters, sons, and daughters around the world and through the continents worldwide. Bless them Father as we are grateful to be so blessed.

In Jesus name, AMEN

I Seal Every Prayer in the Mighty Name of Jesus

Finally my brethren… Be strong in the Lord and in the Power of His Might, and having done all to STAND ! STAND in PRAYER !, believing that you have already won the battle with the word of GOD !, and his anointed Son Christ Jesus !

We hope these prayers will draw you and your life nearer to God, his Son Christ Jesus, our lord and Savior, and the Holy Spirit our Teacher, the Angels our Defenders and to an unwavering faith in God.

Remember… Stay in "Conversation with God, and he will stay in Conversation" with you.

Chief Apostle Dr. J.G. Rice
"I will be Praying for You"

About The Author

Dr. Rice is the founding pastor of the Greater Harvest Christian Center Churches Worldwide (Inc.), which was founded in the year 1992. After Dr. Rice served in the evangelism field for eight years and as a local minister for four years, she was consecrated in the year 2004 as an Apostle in the city of Columbia, South Carolina where she served most of her junior and senior ministerial services. Chief Apostle Rice is the consecrated, elected, and appointed (2009–2015) Chief Apostle to the InterGlobal Association of Christian Churches Worldwide and works daily to insure global unity and pastoral networking to the fivefold ministry and to the body of Christ. Chief Apostle also serves as CEO of Rice Ministries International. This dynamic woman of the Cross is a noted soloist, psalmist and sought after revivalist with the gift of taking the body of Christ through exhortation and worship directly into the throne room of God.

She is the wife of Archbishop James Rice, whom she loves, respects, adores, and knows God sent him to her. She is the biological mother of three gifted, talented, and dedicated-to-God's-Kingdom Kids and the spiritual, Godmother, Mentor, Pastor, Coach, and Apostle to the nations. Bishop and Chief Apostle now grandparents of eight, were both born in Columbia, South Carolina, and now live in South Florida. They pastor Greater Harvest Christian Center Churches Worldwide South also known as GHCC South Florida.

Dr. J. G. Rice is a gift to the world, and to the Body of Christ, she is and has been a successful radio host, television personality, and professional instructor. She is a Chancellor of Harvest University International Bible College and President of West Harvest High School. She has numerous awards, certificates, and honors. Chief Apostle Rice is also a recording artist, and author of over 15 books including "It's All About the Kingdom" and her newly released books "Prayers From the Altar" and "The Transformation Factor." She is both a Teacher, Infuser, Orator, and a powerful Preacher. Dr. Rice is the founder of over 37 ministries, including Greater Harvest Christian Center Churches Worldwide and is Chief Apostle for many InterGlobal Churches. As one educated, she believes in education and promotes actively against violence in her Circle 59' Ministry.

She is a life-changing conference speaker, revivalist, workshop host, and an all-round mentor, coach, and covering to the body of Christ. Apostle believes in Kingdom Living and Kingdom Protocol, and these two things operating in your life will bring a Kingdom blessing that will manifest here on earth. This is a true voice that must be heard in every nation, every city, every town, every house; every ear must hear what the Spirit has to say, through this teaching, preaching, prophetic, Apostolic gift to the church.

Her scripture for life is. "I'm just the voice of one crying in the wilderness, preparing the way of the Lord.—Chief Apostle Dr. J. G. Rice

www.ingramcontent.com/pod-product-compliance
Lightning Source LLC
Chambersburg PA
CBHW060950230426
43665CB00015B/2134